WAR ON DEBT

A.J.Owen

WAR ON DEBT
Copyright © 2013 A.J.Owen

All Rights Reserved

No part of this book may be reproduced in any form, by photocopying or by any electronic or mechanical means, including information storage or retrieval systems, without permission in writing from the copyright owner of this book.

First published December 2013 by
AJBooks, 15 Duchess Road, Monmouth, NP25 3HT

ISBN 978-1-291-64065-6

Printed for AJBooks by Lulu.com

Other books by A J Owen

The Escapades of Mortimer Brown (2006) – spy story,

The Day the Gulf Stream Stopped (2009) – environmental fiction,

So Many False Dawns in British Politics (2010) – political and economic analysis,

On Mr President's Service (2010) – the second Mortimer Brown book

Cover

The front cover illustrates how the UK public debt has increased three-fold over the past 10 years (2003-2013), while industrial output has fallen by approximately 13% – and the gulf is widening dramatically.

Photograph

The photograph on the back cover shows the author with his one-year-old granddaughter, Charlotte.

CONTENTS

p.1   Ch 1:   Introduction

p.4   Ch 2:   The national debt

p.15   Ch 3:   The government deficit

p.24   Ch 4:   Eliminating the budget deficit through government cuts

p.36   Ch 5:   Reducing the deficit through income generation

p.42   Ch 6:   Reducing the deficit through increased taxation

p.51   Ch 7:   Privatisation of public assets

p.60   Ch 8:   Britain's balance of payments deficit

p.71   Ch 9:   Personal debt

p.79   Ch 10: On the inequality of income

p.86   Ch 11: Price inflation

p.91   Ch 12: Monetary reform

p.106 Ch 13: Alternative banking

p.117 Ch 14: A change in public attitude?

WAR ON DEBT

Chapter 1: INTRODUCTION

"When you take a look at the problems our country is facing, debt is No.1. The math is downright scary and the credit markets aren't going to keep on giving us cheap rates." - Paul Ryan (recent Republican nominee for post of US Vice-President)

Preamble

Debt is well known to be a central problem facing many countries today. However, it does not seem to be generally recognised how dangerous the present debt crisis is. To illustrate my point: in the past minute while I composed this sentence, the UK national debt rose by about another £20,000.

Most people seem to think we can probably carry on behaving more or less as we are, but I believe as a country we are heading towards economic meltdown as a result of this. I want us to avert the social disaster which will inevitably result from inaction, before it is too late - which is the reason I have written this book, as a kind of wake-up call for us all to fight against what I shall call the enemy of debt.

I shall be talking mainly about the debt crisis in the UK, but the same problem is prevalent to a greater or lesser extent in virtually all countries in the western capitalist world. It is probably no surprise to learn that the whole sequence of events that took place exacerbating the debt problem here began in the USA when the Wall Street investment bank Lehmans collapsed in September 2008. This event seemed to trigger the global credit crunch and subsequent economic downturn. It was primarily the toxic debt that arose through subprime mortgages in the USA that started the whole financial crisis. The UK was merely mimicking all along the same behaviour, with predictably the same outcome, leading to several UK banks also becoming insolvent. This was tackled by massive government bailouts that added considerably to the country's public debt.

The debt issue in general

The whole issue of debt is, of course, extremely complex. There are many aspects to it, and it would be foolish for me to pretend I can comprehensively explain all of its pros and cons. In this book I more or less treat it on two different levels: one is the level of personal debt, the other is government or national debt. Its importance is indicated by the large number of books that have been written about it; each month a few more appear in the bookshops, such that it is impossible to keep up with them all. The subject of debt also features in a large number of wise quotes which I shall dot about the book.

The academic side of me tells me to define the problem first, before I can hope to set about solving it. So, we need to decide exactly what debt is, and what the problem with it is. Debt is simply defined as money that is owed or due to someone. When we borrow money and thus become in debt there are conditions attached to this: when it has to be repaid and how much additional money has to be paid back as interest.

We therefore lose a certain amount of our freedom in taking out a loan. As Ralph Waldo Emerson, the American essayist and poet, put it: *"A man in debt is so far a slave."* Thus, debt is a form of slavery. If you are indebted to someone, you have to obey certain rules to comply with their requirements. It's essentially the same for governments as it is for individuals. Paying off interest on a debt prevents you from doing other things: for example, one quarter of the UK government's tax revenues are currently swallowed up with just paying off the interest on the national debt, meaning that hospitals, roads, schools, etc. cannot be built, unless even more debt is accrued. Personal debt interest payments mean your disposable income is reduced, so you can't have that holiday or improve your home without adding to your debt. I hope you can see that this is a kind of "vicious spiral": by taking out debt you may indeed be able to build a hospital or a road, but the hospital or road you build will be smaller than or not as good as it would have been if you had managed to save the money first before building it, because you effectively have to sacrifice some of the money you borrowed in order to pay down the debt.

However, a very different view is held in financial circles about the uses or benefits of debt, which is then more euphemistically called credit or borrowing. To illustrate this I shall quote a headline article in *The Telegraph* from December 2008[1]: *"Government must oil the wheels of business to get the country out of recession... The Government's £500 billion recapitalisation has prevented banks from collapsing but credit remains fiendishly tight. The banks say they are lending at similar rates as before but the drying-up of the bond market means businesses need far more credit from them than in the past."*

Here we see debt looked upon as an economic tool to "lubricate" or stimulate the economy. However, not all financiers and politicians necessarily agree entirely with this attitude. For example, the Conservative MEP, Daniel Hannan, has stated that: *"You cannot spend your way out of recession or borrow your way out of debt."*[2]

The more one looks into the issue of debt the more one realises we are all bound up in a global ideological battle. Susan George, the renowned social scientist and activist, once remarked: *"Debt is such a powerful tool, it is such a useful tool, it's much better than colonialism ever was because you can keep control without having an army, without having a whole administration."*

This book will try to expose and deal with some of the implications and consequences for ordinary people of this ideological battle concerning debt, but first of all in the next chapter I would like to present some of the facts and figures relating to our own public debt in the UK - scary they certainly are.

---

[1] http://www.telegraph.co.uk/comment/telegraph-view/3835592/Government-must-oil-the-wheels-of-business-to-lift-the-economy-out-of-recession.html
[2] I am not sure if Daniel Hannan is personally the originator of this well-known quotation

Chapter 2: THE NATIONAL DEBT

"Blessed are the young for they shall inherit the national debt."
- *Herbert Hoover (former US President)*

Preamble

The government is storing up huge debt problems for future generations. Indeed, both government and personal debt have increased over the past few years by an unacceptably large amount. We cannot keep shifting the problem away from us forever. At some point we shall have to face it. Most people seem to be in denial about or unaware of the impending disaster that is going to occur if we do not remedy the situation. Of course, no-one knows exactly when the metaphorical "train crash" will occur, and very few people are prepared for it. You could, however, wake up tomorrow morning to the news that a government gilt auction has failed, share prices have crashed, the country has been declared bankrupt and the value of Sterling has collapsed. You might think that this could not possibly happen, because we will get plenty of warning in advance. Well, actually, we've already had plenty of warning.

So, the country is in debt, companies are in debt, and we as individuals are in debt. We euphemistically call this debt: borrowing, financing, mortgages, hire purchase, leasing, credit, and so on. But the debt has become so large that it is now impossible to bring it under control using conventional means. A radical approach is urgently needed in order to soften the crash when it comes. It is not sufficient for the

Chancellor of the Exchequer just to be fiddling with the economy in his annual budget while Britain burns. Deep-rooted changes are needed.

This chapter is just about the government's debt mountain, called the national debt. I shall discuss personal debt in a subsequent chapter.

What is meant by the national debt?

The national debt is essentially the accumulating budget deficit that will have to be repaid by the government. It is currently rising to heights that in the past were only associated with wartime economic conditions. The rapid rise is quite reminiscent of the situation at the beginning of the 1920s, a few years before the Great Depression. This is a mind-bogglingly overwhelming problem for the country which has to be cracked. It will not just go away.

The national debt (ND) is variously called public debt, government debt or sovereign debt, and is essentially the money owed by central government to the private sector. The official government measure of what is commonly known as the national debt is now called the Public Sector Net Debt (PSND). This refers to the combined debt of central and local government plus the publicly-owned corporations. Measuring the PSND is the joint responsibility of the Office for National Statistics (ONS) and HM Treasury. Depending on exactly how it is defined and what it includes, different figures for the ND can be found in the literature. It is difficult to be entirely consistent, but I shall usually quote figures for the public debt as the total outstanding quantity of money borrowed by the government through the issue of securities by the Treasury and other government agencies.

Government debt as a percentage of GDP

In the first quarter of 2013 the UK government debt amounted to £1.377 trillion (in words, nearly one point four million million pounds). Due to the government's huge budget deficit (which will be discussed in the next chapter) the debt is increasing by approximately £120 billion per annum. Since the population of the UK is about 63.7 million, this represents a debt per capita of nearly £22,000, or in the region of £56,000 per average family household. Just a few years ago, in 2007, the national debt was running at (only) £637 billion or about 43% of the country's annual GDP[3]; in the past six years it has more than doubled to well over one-thousand billion (one trillion pounds) or about 90% of GDP.

One could think of this debt as something similar to a house mortgage or hire-purchase loan, but on a vastly bigger scale. As with a mortgage, interest has to be paid. Using 2009 figures, the government had to pay annual interest on the national debt amounting to about £31 billion (or about £500 per capita or £1,200 per household). In 2012 the interest payments had risen to £43 billion or roughly 3% of GDP. This is roughly the same size as the British defence budget. This means that each household is on average now paying about £1,620 in tax annually just to service the interest payments on the public debt.

History of the national debt

A graph of the way the UK national debt has changed over the past few centuries is shown on the next page. Looked at historically, our present situation does not seem too bad, but you should note that the debt is rising almost vertically at present on the scale of the diagram.

The national debt originated during the reign of King William III (1689-1702). He employed a syndicate of City merchants to offer for sale an issue of government debt. This syndicate soon evolved into the Bank of England, which became established in 1694. The debt revenue was used to finance the wars of the Duke of Marlborough and later Imperial conquests. The national debt increased dramatically during and after the Napoleonic wars at the beginning of the 19th century (1803-1815), rising to over 250% of GDP.

---

[3] GDP = Gross Domestic Product, a measure for the size of the economy

WAR ON DEBT

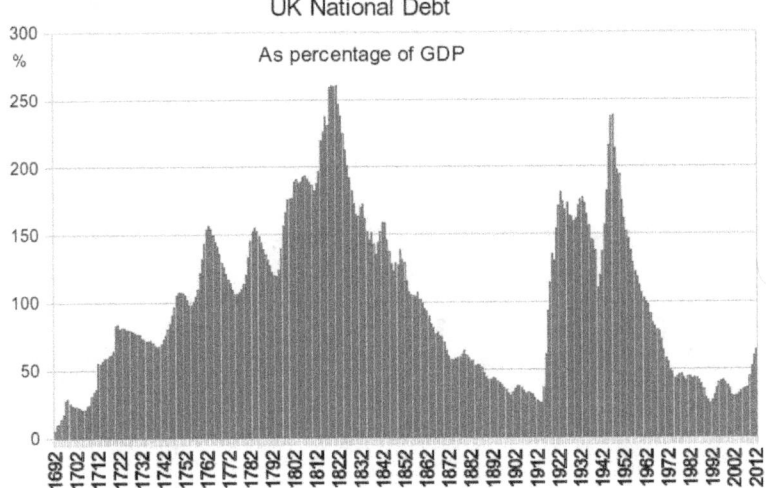

Fig.2.1 United Kingdom National Debt from 1692 - 2012 (attributable to Wikipedia[4])

Then, mainly during the reign of Queen Victoria (1837-1901), the debt fell to about 25% of GDP. After the First World War (WW1) broke out, the debt rose again, to over 150% of GDP. It remained high in the 1920s and 1930s during the Slump and Great Depression, which altogether lasted nearly 20 years. The debt came down slightly in the lead up to the Second World War (WW2) due to increased economic activity, but then - as money was borrowed to fund WW2 and the subsequent recovery programme after the war took place - the national debt rose astronomically to almost 250% of GDP by about 1949 when the country was struggling very seriously. After 1949, partly due to economic recovery and partly due to the American Marshall Aid plan for the rebuilding of Europe, the debt decreased almost exponentially. It wasn't until about 1980 that it had again reached the sort of peacetime level it had had before WW1. From about

---

[4] http://en.wikipedia.org/wiki/File:UK_GDP.png

1980, for many years the national debt was a fairly steady percentage of GDP, between about 30 and 35%.

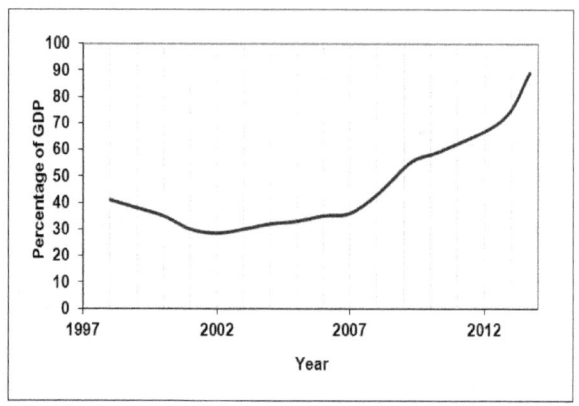

Fig.2.2   *UK National Debt as a percentage of GDP (1998 to 2013)*

On taking office in 1997 Labour inherited a debt of 43.6% of GDP from the Tories. The national debt since the year 1998 is shown in closer detail in the above graph. Labour reduced the debt to 30% of GDP by 2002, but since then a very disturbing trend has reappeared: in 2007 the debt was at 36% of GDP, but by August 2008 it had jumped to 43% of GDP. The deep recession that then occurred caused Alistair Darling as Chancellor to borrow vast amounts of extra money to finance the shortfall between his revenue from taxes and the outgoings required to pay for its public spending programme, together with the financial interventions he made to bail out insolvent banks (see below). At present the national debt has reached about 90% of GDP (according to the CIA World Factbook 2013), still with a strong upwards trend. The government's target of not exceeding 40% of GDP has now been broken very seriously.

WAR ON DEBT

Financial interventions

In the year 2007 financial markets began to enter a period of instability that caused difficulties for banks across the world, precipitating a global credit crisis, a widespread economic downturn and concern over some Eurozone governments being able to pay their debt obligations. The UK Treasury intervened to protect the banks and their depositors. The Treasury's support to the banks included the recapitalisation of Lloyds Banking Group and Royal Bank of Scotland (RBS) through a series of transactions acquiring 83% of RBS, costing the taxpayer £46 billion, and 41% of Lloyds, costing £21 billion. Money was also lent to the Financial Services Compensation Scheme so that it could guarantee customer deposits of up to £50,000. Northern Rock and Bradford & Bingley were nationalised for £117 billion, and a Special Liquidity Scheme was introduced to increase the liquidity of UK banks, costing £200 billion; a Credit Guarantee Scheme was also introduced in October 2008 to help restore investor confidence in bank wholesale funding by guaranteeing certain unsecured debts in return for a fee, plus an Asset Protection Scheme to protect assets on banks' balance sheets. The total level of support provided to banks stood at over £1 trillion, a large proportion of this as guarantees that have not (yet) been called upon. The cost to the taxpayer, however, has been considerable. In the meantime Northern Rock has been sold to Virgin Money. The government is intent on reprivatising RBS and Lloyds, but as yet their market value represents a loss of £28 billion. How much the taxpayer will recoup will depend on a number of different factors, including the eventual proceeds from the disposal of the shareholdings in RBS and Lloyds Banking Group.

In addition to all of this, many analysts claim that the total national debt is even higher than those official figures suggest. This is because national debt should also include pension contributions and private finance initiatives (PFI) which the government are obliged to pay. In addition, the publicly owned rail infrastructure company, Network Rail, has a debt of at least £20 billion which is not officially included in the government's accounts. In 2011 the

Centre for Policy Studies (CPS) argued that the true national debt excluding interventions was already running at 103.5% of GDP. This figure included all the public sector pension liabilities such as pensions and PFI contracts. More recent figures from the CPS (September 2012) show that the ND including financial interventions is 137.5% of GDP. Certainly, whatever one includes in the calculation, the figures are all mind-bogglingly high and unacceptable in the long run.

The link to unemployment

In general, a sharply increasing trend in national debt reflects a deteriorating economic health for the country. When an economy slows and goes into recession, the GDP falls and unemployment rises, which reduces government revenues. As a counter-measure, governments conventionally increase their borrowing in order to try to stimulate the economy and avert the spectre of high employment.

In October 2008 unemployment stood at 1.79 million or 5.7% of the workforce (prior to the most recent recession). By December 2008 it had risen to 1.97 million or 6.3%, and in October 2009 it reached 2.49 million or 7.6%. The upward trend has fortunately, and perhaps unexpectedly, now levelled off according to official figures which indicated an unemployment figure of 2.49 million in September 2013, even though job losses in manufacturing industries are being announced in the news on a daily basis. According to Mr Osborne's latest forecast in his Autumn Statement of 5th December 2013, unemployment is predicted to fall to 7.0% by 2015 and back to 5.6% by 2018 if the current return to economic growth remains sustained.

The unemployment figure has recently come into the limelight as now being a criterion which the Bank of England will use in future to determine its base lending rate. The new Governer of the BoE, Mark Carney, has made it clear that the Monetary Policy Committee (MPC) will only consider changing (viz. increasing) the bank rate, if and when the unemployment figure drops below 7%. This policy of "forward guidance" is intended to bring stability to the lending market.

WAR ON DEBT

Other countries' debts

It provides no real consolation to learn that the UK is not the worst culprit regarding the relative size of its public debt. Recent figures issued by the *CIA* and *Eurostat* are shown below for a selection of the world's important economies. Using a debt to GDP ratio is one of the most accepted ways of assessing a nation's debt. For example, in theory, one of the criteria of admission to the European Union's currency is that a country's debt does not exceed 60% of its GDP.[5]

National Debt as a percentage of GDP

	(July 2011)	*(most recent)*
Japan	226	214
Greece	144	161
Iceland	124	96
Italy	118	126
Ireland	94	126
France	84	90
Portugal	83	120
Germany	79	82
UK	**77**	**89**
Spain	63	85
USA	59	74
(World average)	59	64
China	18	32
Russia	10	12

Nearly all the countries listed above have had a large increase in their percentage of debt over the past few years. Of these selected countries, only Russia is managing to keep its government debt to a moderate level.

This is not the whole story, however, because countries also possess external financial assets offsetting their debts, and it is the difference between their external assets and their debts that is a

---

[5] http://en.wikipedia.org/wiki/Government_debt

significant measure of a country's real economic strength or weakness. This is expressed in an economic index called the Net International Investment Position (NIIP), also listed below as a percentage of GDP for several countries. A plus sign essentially means a country is gaining in wealth, whereas a minus sign indicates decreasing wealth. From this list we can see which countries have an inherently strong economy, and which countries do not. In a nutshell, Switzerland is a safe haven for financial investment. Norway, with a very small population, is benefiting greatly from the wealth gained from its huge North Sea oil and gas extraction industry. Japan, Germany and China are generating huge wealth from the surplus they gain from exporting manufactured goods. Belgium is a surprise candidate for a healthy position. It has been suggested ironically that Belgium's economic health has come about because the country has had no effective government interfering with its economy for almost two years (during 2010 and 2011)!

Net International Investment Position (% of GDP)

Country	NIIP	Year
Switzerland	+136.1	(2010)
Norway	+95.8	(2010)
Belgium	+66.6	(2012)
Japan	+56.1	(2009)
Netherlands	+50.9	(2012)
Germany	+40.5	(2012)
China	+37.1	(2009)
Russia	+17.9	(2009)
UK	**- 9.1**	**(2012)**
France	- 18.8	(2011)
USA	- 16.9	(2010)
Italy	- 20.7	(2011)
Spain	- 91.4	(2012)
Rep.of Ireland	- 95.8	(2012)
Greece	-114.1	(2012)
Portugal	-116.5	(2012)

WAR ON DEBT

The countries with a negative sign are essentially living beyond their means. Until recently Mr Sarkozy was battling to reduce France's debt, which is allegedly caused by the deeply engrained easy life that France's civil servants and public employees are accustomed to. In the UK, Mr Osborne is now in the process of trying to reduce the UK's budget deficit against the backdrop of high welfare, health and education costs coupled with insufficient tax revenue. In the USA, the government has essentially hedged the issue by increasing the amount of money that the government is allowed to borrow. Finally, it is no surprise that some Eurozone countries, such as Italy, Greece, Spain, Ireland and Portugal, which are in danger of defaulting on their government debts, come at the bottom of this list. For comparison, I have also listed below the total external debt in terms of debt per capita (converted to US dollars) for a selection of important countries. I think the figures speak for themselves. The UK's residents have almost the greatest debt of all countries listed. Only the Republic of Ireland's residents are in a worse situation.

External Debt per capita (in US Dollars)

Republic of Ireland	503,914
UK	**144,338**
France	74,619
Germany	57,755
Greece	47,636
Spain	47,069
Portugal	46,795
USA	45,097
Italy	36,841
Japan	19,148
Russia	3,421
China	303

Conclusion

Successive UK governments have not been able to keep our national debt at a sensibly moderate level, let alone eliminate it in a situation when as a country we have plenty of wealth and are not struggling with war or famine. At present just the interest payments are consuming 3% of our national product, without paying off any of the debt. This can only improve when the budget deficit has been eliminated entirely and an annual surplus regularly achieved. The sooner this is effected the better, since we cannot rely indefinitely on interest rates on the debt being as low as they are now. A long period of austerity is likely to be necessary, in order that our children and grandchildren do not have to carry an excessive burden of debt in the future. However, there are other possibilities, not necessarily condemning us all to decades of austere misery. Amongst other things, we require a radical overhaul of the monetary system – which will inevitably be resisted by the current establishment of politicians, bankers and financiers – as well as a change in public attitude towards debt. These topics will be discussed in subsequent chapters.

Chapter 3: THE GOVERNMENT DEFICIT

"Britain has no divine right to be one of the richest countries in the world." - George Osborne, UK Chancellor of the Exchequer

Preamble

This chapter deals with the government's fiscal or budget deficit. The Coalition Government and Labour Opposition disagree about the timing of debt reduction and the extent to which it should be carried out. The Coalition has been attempting an immediate deficit reduction via government cuts plus low interest rates to stimulate the economy, whereas Labour believes essentially that we should wait until the economy has recovered before imposing cuts. The whole argument involves considerable polemic around the issue of whether cuts may be counter-productive by stifling economic growth, which would then mean that the deficit could increase due to a reduction in tax revenues and increased benefit pay-outs.

In any case, however, if the government deficit is not eliminated soon, the national debt will at some point in the future inevitably spiral out of control. Thus, we are metaphorically waiting for a "high-speed train crash" to occur. Do we close our eyes and wait for the impact, or do we perhaps jump off the train and try to save our own skin? Alternatively, do we try to do something about it for everyone's sake – by getting into the driver's cab and applying the brakes? First of all, let us look at some of the figures.

The UK budget deficit

Successive UK governments have nurtured the attitude of keeping taxes low. Tax revenues are then insufficient to fulfil the government's spending commitments, so each year the government runs up a large budget deficit. The money that isn't raised by taxation or by selling off public assets has to be borrowed, and every year this budget deficit is added to our national debt. For example, in the financial year 2009-10, the last Labour government spent £671.4 billion, despite tax revenues of only £496.1 billion, which amounted to a deficit of £175.3 billion.

In the next graph I have plotted the UK's budget deficit in money terms over the calendar years from 1975 to 2012 (not corrected for inflation). A budget deficit is plotted upwards. In this representation, the peak in the deficit in 2010 looks much worse than when it is plotted as a percentage of the size of the economy (see Fig.3.2), which gives a better picture of the relative importance of the current deficit. However, we still see that the peak in 2010 is historically the worst it has been within living memory, at 11% of GDP.

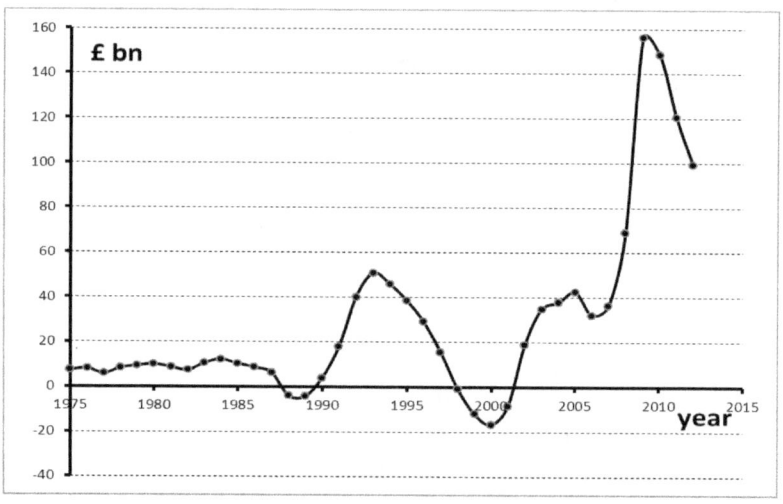

Fig. 3.1 Annual UK Government deficit (1975 - 2012) in £ billion

Overall it has been fairly rare for a budget to be in surplus (negative values in the above graph). Only 1988 and 1989, as well as from 1998 to 2001, show a surplus. When the UK went into recession in the early 1990s, the deficit rose to a historical high of about £50 billion (or 8% of GDP) with John Major as prime minister. However, when Kenneth Clarke took over as his Chancellor of the Exchequer he managed to reduce the deficit to being almost balanced again by 1997.

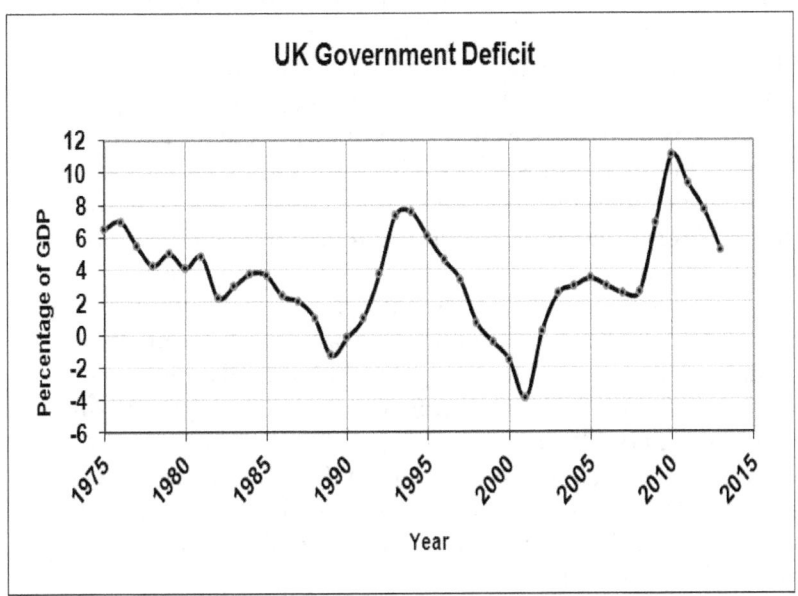

Fig. 3.2 UK Government deficit as a percentage of GDP

The Conservatives lost the general election in 1997, and New Labour under Tony Blair took over the positive trend. Gordon Brown as Chancellor really did seem to be acting "prudently" for a few years, and the budget showed a surplus for about three years. Then, in 2002, the government again "went into the red". For the next 6 years with Gordon Brown as Chancellor, the government held the deficit just at the limit of what is termed the "Maastricht Treaty's Excessive Debt Procedure", which sets the maximum allowed deficit (for all EU countries) at 3% of GDP. Subsequently, when Gordon Brown took over as Prime Minister in 2007 and Alistair Darling became Chancellor – exacerbated by the financial crisis and subsequent recession – caution seemed to go by the wind. They "took out the country's credit card and let rip", such that by the end of the 2009-10 financial year the UK's annual budget deficit had risen to the above mentioned figure of about 11% of GDP.

I should mention that the currency crisis afflicting the Eurozone would not have arisen if European governments had not flouted the Maastricht Treaty's 3% deficit maximum rule, which was laid down to prevent such a crisis occurring in the first place. Surely the politicians who were responsible for allowing excess deficit to occur in their respective countries should be severely castigated, if not put on trial for acting illegally, because this profligacy has seriously undermined the credibility of the common European currency.

Only now are we beginning to see whether the Conservative-led coalition government's measures are having their desired impact of reducing the deficit. For the calendar year 2011 the deficit was £121.9 billion or approximately 9.3% of GDP, an improvement on both 2009 and 2010. For 2012, the figures show the deficit was running at just under 8% of GDP, and for the first 3 quarters of 2013 at between 5 and 6%, which is certainly a reassuring trend in the correct direction. The national debt is still rising all the time, of course!

At the beginning of the parliamentary term Mr Osborne pledged to achieve fiscal sustainability, i.e. elimination of the deficit, by the year 2015, which now seems to be an impossible goal. Since we are not getting there quickly enough currently, the Chancellor has announced further cuts and some measures to obtain extra revenue, e.g., from 2014 the bank levy will rise to 0.156% and from 2015 capital gains tax will be imposed on non-residents selling property in the UK. The Office for Budget Responsibility now forecasts that it will take until the 2018-19 tax year to reach the goal of a balanced fiscal budget. In the next few tax years government borrowing is forecast to drop, as follows: in 2013-14 to £111 bn; 2014-15 to £96 bn; 2015-16 to £79 bn; 2016-17 to £51 bn; 2017-18 to £23 bn; 2018-19 a small surplus.

WAR ON DEBT

How and why does the government borrow money?

To meet the budget deficit, the government borrows money by selling bonds, called gilts. A bond is in principle like a piece of paper with *IOU* written on it! These bonds are sold at regular auctions held by the UK Debt Management Office (DMO), on behalf of the Treasury. The term gilt is short for "gilt-edged security", and is a reference to their perceived safety as an investment. When a gilt is sold by the government, it guarantees to pay the purchaser a fixed amount of interest every six months until the maturity date, at which point the original capital value of the gilt is repaid in full to the purchaser.

These bonds are repayable on average within 15 years, but currently the government can only make the required repayments by selling even more gilts. This procedure, if carried out by a private individual, would be deemed illegal, since it could be likened to a so-called *Ponzi* scheme.[6]

The DMO publishes a quarterly report that shows who owns the UK's debt. Although the majority of gilts are held by British institutions, the amount held overseas has risen sharply since 2003, so that currently just over 35% of our national debt is owed to foreign governments and investors.

Since government borrowing increases the total demand for credit in the economy, it tends to drive up the cost of borrowing for private companies who want to finance investment in equipment, stock and other capital goods. This harms the ability of the private sector to create the wealth and jobs that are needed for economic recovery. In addition, the government needs to sell its bonds at attractive interest rates to entice investors away from alternatives, a phenomenon known as the "crowding out" of private capital.

The government relies on investors being willing to buy UK gilts, but if the bond market becomes nervous about our

---

[6] A Ponzi scheme is a fraudulent investment that pays returns to its investors from their own money or that paid by subsequent investors, rather than from profit earned by the individual or organization running the operation. The system is destined to collapse because the earnings, if any, are less than the payments to investors.

excessive borrowing and ability to repay the loans (as has been the case for the gilts of several other EU countries recently), the demand for gilts falls, and their price declines as a result. Since they now cost less to buy, gilt yields start to rise, which means we pay more in interest for every pound borrowed, and everything from trade finance to mortgage payments gets more expensive. Many of our biggest customers are pension funds and foreign central banks that only invest in the safest, so-called triple-A bonds. Until February 2013 the UK enjoyed this best credit rating possible, but then the credit rating agencies Moody and Fitch downgraded the UK to AA+ owing to the perceived weakened economic outlook, which means that big investors may begin to baulk at buying UK government gilts. Nevertheless, countries such as the USA and France are in the same position.[7]

In addition, the Bank of England (BoE) has been injecting money into the economy via the quantitative easing (QE) programme, which it uses to buy back its own gilts. This risky debauching of Sterling raises the spectre of high inflation once the economy begins to recover. If investors do see their holdings devalued by QE they will be reluctant to buy UK gilts in future, which could send interest rates spiraling upwards. If the government then fails to get a grip on spending and injects even more money to cover the shortfall in gilt sales, extreme inflation and a potentially fatal Sterling crisis would ensue. If a gilt auction were to fail, the country would be plunged into a major economic crisis, similar to, but on a much bigger scale than, that experienced recently by Greece. As a result, Sterling could plummet on the international currency markets, and we might need an IMF bailout to stave off complete bankruptcy. This may sound excessively melodramatic, but it has happened before within living memory, when James Callaghan was Prime Minister in the 1970s.

Consume or produce

Put simplistically, the government spends money for two principal reasons: either to consume or to produce. The most obvious form

---

[7] It was announced on 8/11/2013 that France had been downgraded to AA.

of government consumption is when the state transfers money to people in the form of pensions and benefits. When this money is spent by the government, it sees no direct return on the investment. Alternatively, when the government spends money productively by investing in capital infrastructure, such as roads, railways, energy generation and communication networks, this is likely to bring higher economic output. This type of investment can help to facilitate trade and promote economic activity in the private sector too, where (allegedly) a nation's wealth is created. In other words, borrowing to produce can pay for itself.

The Coalition has, however, as part of its cuts, abandoned some – but not all – of the potentially productive spending projects. The previously proposed third runway at Heathrow Airport is one of them. Secondly, the Severn barrage scheme to produce renewable electricity and create a new road crossing between Wales and the West of England – at an estimated cost of perhaps £30 billion for the most ambitious barrage scheme – has also been dropped for the time being. The proposed 16 km dam stretching from near Weston-super-mare in Somerset to Lavernock in South Wales would incorporate turbines so that it functioned as a tidal power station capable of producing at least 5% of the UK's electricity requirements. The then Energy Secretary Chris Huhne announced in October 2010 that a feasibility study carried out by the Department of Energy and Climate Change had found no strategic case for the scheme. Instead, he announced eight potential sites for building new nuclear power stations by 2025, which will be built and run by a consortium involving foreign companies. It has just been announced, in October 2013, that a new nuclear power station is to be built at Hinckley Point in Somerset using Chinese and French technology. The uncomfortable point about this is that the government has committed us to purchasing electricity from this future power station for the next 50 years at a price which is currently almost double the present price of electricity. In addition, personally I cannot understand why the government allows foreign companies to import nuclear technology large-scale into Britain when British companies should be perfectly capable of designing and constructing nuclear power stations themselves. This "bargain, off-the-shelf" attitude of British governments is crippling our industry, as well as being very bad strategically.

The Thameslink programme, which is a government-funded £6 billion project to introduce new and improved railway stations, track, new cross-London routes, and longer and more frequent trains, is to be continued to completion. However, the government has again not "got the message" regarding the need to safeguard jobs in the British manufacturing industry and, instead of awarding the contract for rolling stock to the Derby-based offshoot of the Canadian company Bombardier, has awarded it to Siemens of Germany. The controversy over this decision, which could lead to an estimated 20,000 job losses in total in the UK, is not yet over.

Furthermore, the government has set up a company called *High Speed 2* to carry out consultative work on the possibility of building a high-speed rail network initially connecting London with the West Midlands, and including a connection to Heathrow airport. The line would then continue as two spurs, one to Manchester and the other to Leeds. The overall cost of this project, which seems to be rising every minute, has now reached about £42 billion. The firm KPMG have analysed the economic benefits of the project, and published a report (September 2013) in which it was stated that this improvement in infrastructure would benefit the UK economy by about £15 billion. Shortly afterwards they were forced to admit via a freedom of information request that benefits for the North and the Midlands would be offset somewhat by large disadvantages for Wales, the South West of England, East Anglia and the North East of Scotland.

Conclusion

Anyone who has to budget – ranging from private householders, through to treasurers of associations, charities and businesses, and also the government's Chancellor of the Exchequer – knows that their main principle and responsibility is always to balance their budget. This essential rule has been broken for decades by government chancellors. Currently it is more important than ever that the government's budget deficit is eliminated, because continued overspending is storing up untold damage to the economy and the lives and well-being of our citizens for many years to come. Politicians who promote increased government spending in order to be popular, without first ensuring a commensurate increase in revenue, are behaving in a wholly irresponsible way.

Chapter 4: REDUCING THE BUDGET DEFICIT THROUGH GOVERNMENT CUTS

"It's not easy cutting welfare bills. It's not easy cutting the deficit." - George Osborne

Preamble

This chapter touches on the subject of the UK government's fiscal deficit, and how at least some of it may be reduced via government cuts. Much of what I shall write could be described as anecdotal, i.e., I shall give some examples that are not meant to be comprehensive at all, but merely give an indication of the sorts of problems there are and how I think they might be addressed.

The legacy from the last government

In the last year of the Brown regime the annual government deficit averaged £14.6 billion/month (£175.3 billion in the tax year 2009-10). This is such an eye-wateringly large amount of money that it is difficult to comprehend the magnitude of it. It means that the government was spending on average £240 per month too much on each individual in our society, or about £620 per average household. Of that, approximately one quarter disappeared totally unproductively as interest on the previously accrued national debt. In accordance with what desperately needs to be done now, the present government is indeed implementing "deficit correction measures" as a priority. These involve mainly a combination of government cuts to the public service and tax changes.

Government cuts and the NHS

At the beginning of the legislature period Mr Osborne announced cuts of £81 billion over this session of parliament (until 2015), which has meant that government departments all over the UK have been instructed to make appropriate savings.

Let us take a fairly concrete example. The Welsh Assembly Government (WG), as a result of the planned cuts, will now receive less money from central government. It consequently ordained that the health boards in Wales, for which it has overall responsibility, were required to save £455.7 million in 2011. This of course caused fear for the quality and quantity of patient care in Wales. A few official suggestions for where the savings could be made were mooted, including efficiency savings (e.g. better IT), a recruitment freeze (in other words, ultimately employing fewer staff), a change in the way the service operates (healthcare in the community rather than in hospital; more centralisation of some services), and the closure of some services altogether. The above suggestions, by their very nature, will undoubtedly involve managerial meddling in the service that will create a lot of added angst and uncertainty amongst the staff. This is not what should happen. Improving IT will certainly cost more money in the short term, rather than less; fewer staff will mean less personal patient care and more overload for the existing staff; changing the operating modus will probably just transfer costs elsewhere, rather than reducing them; and closing services will simply mean a deterioration in the service. To be honest, this all sounds pretty bleak, since the service provided by the hospitals in Wales already leaves much to be desired.

So, how does one cut costs in the health service, whilst maintaining the standard of the service, or even improving it? The short answer is that you don't. You look, amongst other things, for ways to generate income that will help plug the funding gap. This will be discussed in the next chapter.

<u>Cuts via the legal system</u>

The third pillar of democracy, other than the legislature (Parliament) and the executive (Cabinet), is the judiciary. The government shouldn't really influence the workings of the judiciary. However, influence on the justice system may have to be brought by the government, since judges are having a considerable social impact by the way they deal with criminals, and there is also considerable scope for saving large amounts of taxpayers' money.

Shockingly, Britain now has the largest prison population per capita of any country in western Europe. In England and Wales this figure increased under New Labour from about 60,000 in 1997 to 85,000 in 2010. Just in one week during the August 2011 riots it increased by 723 to 86,654.

Looking at the list of offences for which people have been committed to prison, I am left wondering whether judges have not over-reacted in a large number of cases. For example, a 23 year-old university student from London stole a case of bottled water worth £3.50 in the wave of recent rioting - and was given a prison sentence of 6 months; an 18 year-old from Manchester entered looted shops, picked up, but dropped, trainers, drank stolen champagne - and was committed to two years and four months in a youth offenders institution; and a 48 year-old man from Manchester took doughnuts from a looted shop - and was given a prison sentence of 16 months.[8]

I cannot see the sense, frankly, of imprisoning feckless people, such as those mentioned in the above examples, who had a "moment of madness". In my estimation there is really no justification for giving a custodial sentence to anyone who is not really a danger to society – in the sense of whether they are likely to harm anyone physically or mentally. There are literally thousands of people in Britain's prisons at present who have committed non-violent crimes, such as fraud or perjury, and some motoring offences. I have never understood why, for instance, Lord Archer should have been imprisoned for what he did, although I do not condone it. His crime of perjury would surely have been better atoned for if he had been stripped of his peerage and been made to pay a substantial fine to the Crown.

A further example is the tragic case of a lorry driver who fell asleep at the wheel of his vehicle and killed a family in their car. He spent a considerable time in prison for a crime that cannot

---

[8] Source: "Riot convictions: How tough are they?" by Dominic Casiani BBC News website 19th August 2011

really be atoned for, but he could have been fined instead and been required to pay a percentage of any future salary he earned to the close relatives of the bereaved. His misdemeanor was not the sort of crime where a custodial sentence is appropriate, for it was a "technical" crime, i.e., an accident or error of judgement, and in no way would he have wanted to do this on purpose, nor is he likely to do anything similar again.

Furthermore, two-thirds of young men who have been given prison sentences are re-convicted within two years of their release. Surely this statistic tells us something about the failings of our overcrowded prison system, and suggests that imprisonment isn't necessarily the correct solution?

Hence it appears that there needs to be a reappraisal of the function and efficacy of the prison service. Why do judges imprison so many young people when they really require re-education, community service and a large fine to teach them the value of other people's property? This would be a much better punishment, and one that would save the taxpayer money. In other words, since it is very expensive keeping people locked up, there is no sense in imprisoning people when they can be much more useful to their relatives and society outside prison.

For those criminals who are actually a danger to society and should be locked up, why cannot the prison system actually pay for itself through useful work that they could do while they are inside prison? Shouldn't they pay for their board and lodgings, like everyone else in society, and be required to do some kind of worthwhile job? Prisons should be regarded and run as a form of educational establishment which has to be funded by the people who use it, i.e., prisoners should be required to pay fees, similar to the way students have to pay fees for their higher education at university. Convicted criminals should also have to recompense their victims and pay the costs of their court case. Surely this would be a major deterrent to re-offending. There is no reason why they shouldn't be required to pay back the costs over several years like a loan, just as university students have to do via the Student Loan Company.

The doubter will obviously say that criminals will only steal more money to repay their fines, and that imprisonment works as a deterrent. Moreover the policy "tough on crime and punishment" is always a vote-winner. However, spells in prison do not seem to have a reforming effect on most criminals anyway; prisons seem to be places where there is a regime of bullying, and where young offenders learn even more sophisticated methods of criminality. The Director of the Howard League for Penal Reform, Frances Crook, said recently: *"Every week we cram hundreds more people into our already bulging jails, only for people to leave prison unchanged and to go back to crime. Prisons are awash with drugs, violence and arson and this is inflicted on local communities when people leave prison. The answer to rising prison populations is not to build more failing jails. This ceaseless growth in prison numbers is untenable and I implore the government to bite the bullet and find a strategic way to reduce the prison population by putting an end to short term prison sentences. A record prison high is a sign of failure, not success."* [9] It therefore seems obvious to me that a great deal of taxpayers' money could be saved, and society spared a lot of misery, if judges did not imprison young offenders and non-violent criminals so readily.

Meanwhile, the public have been trying to understand why the unrest in the summer of 2011 should have occurred at all. One youth worker interviewed on radio claimed that "poverty" was the cause of the wanton violence, while the leader of the Headteachers' Union, Brian Lightman, made the point that "There need to be some hard questions and uncomfortable truths for parents and families." Mr Lightman blamed a toxic mixture of disfunctional parenting and a consumer and celebrity culture, which tells youngsters they should have whatever they want. He warned that *"Too often, schools are faced with pupils who have never had any boundaries in their home lives, and where there has never been a sense of right and wrong".*

Another shocking statistic is that 10% of the prison population are ex-servicemen. These are mostly young men who have served their country by being sent by politicians into

[9] Source http://www.bbc.co.uk/news/uk-14252315

dangerous war zones such as Afghanistan and Iraq. Many of them return home traumatised and disorientated in society. Surely, it is time that politicians realised we should not be doing this to our young men and women in a modern civilised society? Just from a materialistic standpoint, enormous amounts of money could be saved by bringing our servicemen and women home, and thus cutting out the unnecessary deaths and physical or mental disabilities inflicted on them in campaigns whose justification is highly questionable. This brings us to the proposed defence cuts.

Defence cuts

Defence is a huge topic about which one could write several tomes, but I just want to mention a few points here briefly. The defence cuts announced by the Coalition in the autumn of 2010 include the premature decommissioning of The Ark Royal and the axing of the fleet of Harrier jets, which means that Britain will have no capability for flying fixed-wing planes from aircraft carriers until the year 2019. The then Defence Secretary Liam Fox told the BBC - using a rather unconvincing argument - that there had been periods in the past, before the Harriers came on stream, when the UK had aircraft carriers with no planes to fly on them. He added that there would be a range of helicopters and unmanned aircraft which would still be able to fly from them. Also, strike fighter aircraft from allies like France would be able to land on UK aircraft carriers, and vice versa.

I am inclined to agree with the Opposition leader Ed Milliband in this particular instance, who said that the defence review was a "missed opportunity". Mr Milliband claimed: "It is a spending review dressed up as a defence review; it has been chaotically conducted; it has been hastily prepared and it is simply not credible as a strategic blueprint for our future defence needs."

The problems with Britain's defence procurement, however, go back many years to well before the time of Mr Cameron, Dr Fox and Mr Milliband. Over decades, the UK has been allowing itself to become increasingly dependent on the USA for its military equipment. For example, one of the major turning points occurred in 1960, when Britain's intended nuclear deterrent using the British designed and built Blue Streak missile was scrapped, soon culminating in Britain turning to the Americans for their submarine-based Polaris system as a replacement nuclear deterrent. Subsequently, Polaris was replaced by the Trident submarine-based system that we have today. As the existing Trident system gradually ages, the policy has been to delay the issue of replacing it as long as possible and to try to cut costs by reducing the number of warheards to be deployed in the missiles. Mr Cameron hopes to save £750 million in this way and to defer the final spending decision until 2016, which is after the next general election. The Lib Dems, before the last election, wanted to reduce the deterrent to two-thirds of its present capability, but no major political party now has the courage to want to scrap it entirely, even though it will cost in the region of £20 billion to replace over several years.

To remind the reader: Trident is essentially a weapon that can never be used. It is unthinkable that the UK government would unilaterally give the go-ahead to fire any of its nuclear missiles at targets in any other country. Nevertheless, one could argue that Trident is serving its purpose successfully, since there has been no direct attack on the UK from an external aggressor since we have possessed this deterrent.[10] On the other hand, if any "rogue nation" did attack the UK with nuclear weapons or otherwise, NATO forces, in particular those from the USA, would undoubtedly retaliate, in order to defend Britain, with whatever means they felt necessary.

Next, we could take the example of the Harrier jump jet. This is an aircraft capable of vertical take-off and landing (VTOL) that was originally designed and built in the UK in the 1960s. It became modified and updated over the years. By the 1980s the Harrier II was being manufactured both in the USA by McDonnell Douglas (Boeing) and in the UK by British Aerospace. Control over the development and manufacture of the Harrier

---

[10] This is rather like elephant powder. It's essential to buy some, since, if you sprinkle it in your garden, you will be guaranteed to have no elephants trampling all over your vegetables

diminished over the years (as is typical for any good idea that comes out of the UK), and when it was becoming clear that the Harrier was coming to the end of its lifetime in the USA, the so-called Joint Strike Fighter programme was set up there in 1993 as a development and acquisition program intended to replace a wide range of existing fighter, strike and ground attack aircraft. The UK joined the programme formally in 1995 with a stake of 10% in the project, and a contribution of $2.5 billion to the development costs. Two American companies vied for the contract, and eventually Lockheed-Martin was chosen over Boeing to produce a plane that has become known as the F35 Lightning II. The UK will be buying a variant of these planes to replace the Harrier jump jets on Britain's new Queen Elizabeth Class aircraft carriers. The planes will be manufactured and assembled in the USA, with the UK company BAE Systems providing quite a few of the components. Clearly, this is better than nothing, but it is a far cry from the days when the UK designed and built its own aircraft in their entirety.

There has been a huge amount of debate over the above-mentioned Queen Elizabeth class aircraft carriers, which were originally commissioned by the previous Labour government. One of the problems was that when Labour were voted out of office they left behind a £38 billion "black hole" in the defence budget, i.e., signed contracts without properly securing the funding. Inheriting this situation, the coalition government found that if they had wanted to cancel the aircraft carriers, in order to save money, it would have been more expensive to do this than to have the ships built to completion. In addition, in order to be able to pay for the new F35 Joint Strike Fighters that will use the aircraft carriers, the government has had to sacrifice the existing fleet of Harrier jump jets.

But we haven't finished yet: BAE Systems had also been developing a military surveillance plane, Nimrod MRA4, which was intended to be the successor to the Nimrod MR2, phased out in March 2010, which has three main roles: anti-submarine warfare, anti-surface unit warfare and search and rescue. Its range enables the crew to monitor maritime areas far to the north of

Iceland and up to 4,000 km out into the Western Atlantic. The MR2 was a "submarine killer" carrying sensors and data processing equipment linked to weapon systems. The original Hawker Siddley Nimrod was developed and built in the UK from 1964, and based on a modification of the de Havilland Comet, the world's first jet airliner. It was originally designed by de Havilland's successor, Hawker Siddley, now part of BAE Systems, and used as a Royal Air Force maritime patrol aircraft. The Nimrod MRA4 was essentially a new aircraft, with current-generation Rolls Royce BR210 turbofan engines, capable of in-flight refuelling (as was needed during the 1982 Falklands War), as well as having "hardpoints" to allow it to carry missiles.

However, the Nimrod MRA4 project was subject to delays, cost over-runs, and contract re-negotiations. As a result of the Strategic Defence and Security Review, it was cancelled in 2010, at which point it was £789 million over budget and nine years late. (Better late than never, I would say!) The three prototype aircraft, produced at a cost of over £1 billion each, have now been scrapped.

The cancellation of Nimrod MRA4 is surely a serious blow to the British aircraft industry, and dangerous for Britain's defence capabilities. The scientific, economic, social, political and military repercussions of the cancellation could be immensely damaging, which raises serious questions about the competence of the decision-making that has been going on. If there is a defence need for the aircraft - which there certainly is - then it should not be cancelled. Over-running the target date is actually no real disadvantage, because the end product will probably be an improvement; over-running the costing on such a long-term project is also not that unusual or important for such a product that does not bring in any returns on the investment in any case. Compared to the hundreds of billions of pounds that the previous Labour government recently gave to irresponsible banks, the budget over-run on Nimrod is quite insignificant!

Here are some further interesting defence statistics. According to *The Mail Online* (June 2010), Whitehall has revealed figures showing that fighting the wars in Afghanistan and

Iraq alongside the USA has cost British taxpayers more than £20 billion since the 9/11 terror attacks in 2001. This total does not even include the salaries of soldiers or paying for their long-term injuries and mental health care, and it is in addition to the UK's £35 billion annual defence budget.

The politicians in conjunction with the military have obviously decided to agree that the deployment of British troops in Afghanistan is necessary for the defence and/or security of the UK, but I must admit that I cannot really see how this can actually be the case. I am sure that the majority of people in Britain feel the same way as I do, that this extra expense of around £2 billion annually is something we cannot afford, and should not be spending.

The plan is for the Afghans themseves to take over the security of their country step-by-step, of course, and then Britain should be able to withdraw its troops by the year 2015. The former Defence Secretary, Liam Fox, announced (August 2011), however, that the Ministry of Defence has signed a contract to purchase "off the shelf" 14 new Chinook helicopters from the American company Boeing at a cost of approximately £1 billion. There is surely a certain illogicality about this decision, since the extra Chinooks - which are needed to transport troops and equipment around Afghanistan - will only start to be delivered by the end of 2014, when most of Britain's troops will have been withdrawn from there anyway. This seems to me to be a lot of taxpayers' money being spent on helicopters that will probably not be needed for the rôle for which they were originally envisaged.

Local government cuts

Nearer to home, the effect of government cuts in spending is being passed on to local authorities. My own County Council in Monmouthshire has recently been holding public meetings to inform the public of the impending cuts and gain some public support for the proposed measures through a process of open and transparent democracy. Having been told that £23 million has to be saved over the next three years, we were asked what services we thought should be cut. We are talking about relatively small amounts of money here: the annual net average cost of running a library is £312,000, and the cost of running a leisure centre is £461,000, for example. Closing the local library and leisure centre would only bring minor savings for the council, but quite major disadvantages for the public. In my opinion, which I expressed at the meeting, it would be better for the Council to raise some revenue directly to cover those costs: an entrance fee, parking fee, borrowing fee, etc. There is no point in closing down important educational and recreational public services for the sake of a small amount of money, when they could be part-financed fairly easily by the people actually using them.

Finally, something that hardly ever gets factored into the costs properly: if you close down a public service, you put people out of work. These people are then unemployed, at least for a while, and could probably cost the public purse in social security benefits almost as much as the amount of money saved. Secondly, there is an unquantifiable benefit in keeping a library and leisure centre open: the public are more educated and healthy as a result. This must surely be beneficial: educated and fit people are more effective at creating wealth for the community, and they cost the health service less money in the long run. My plea would therefore be, *not* to cut public services and hope the private sector will "take up the slack". Minor cuts like these are counter-productive.

Conclusion

To eliminate the budget deficit by 2015 via government cuts alone is too much of a tall order for the Chancellor. More cuts to defence could have deleterious effects on our national security, for example. This chapter has shown that some government savings could still be made, however, via changes to local services, without jeopardising the quality of that service, and by certain measures that could be adopted by the legal system. In his autumn statement on December 5th 2012 Mr Osborne announced, amongst other things, new cuts of several billion pounds via a "benefit squeeze" and some behind-the-scenes cuts in government office costs. Local government cuts are being imposed "from above", causing uncertainty and heartache for local communities; it would be better to raise some revenue locally to pay for the public services in jeopardy, as well as raise council tax by enough to cover more than just the effects of inflation.

Chapter 5: REDUCING THE DEFICIT GAP THROUGH INCOME GENERATION

"Don't go around saying the world owes you a living; the world owes you nothing: it was here first." - Mark Twain (1835 - 1910)

Preamble

There are four different strategies the Chancellor could utilise in order to reduce the deficit; I believe the government should try to obtain a fair balance between them all. Having discussed cuts in the previous chapter, this chapter deals with the way the government could generate income by acting in a more commercially savvy manner. The examples will be restricted here purely to the health service in Wales, but could in principle apply to any area of public spending.

Prescription charges

Some parts of this book are written from a Welsh perspective. For example, Welsh Labour politicians made what I regard to be a financially naïve mistake in 2007 when they abolished prescription charges. In the meantime England is the only country of the UK to continue with such charges, currently costing patients £7.65 per prescription. This amount just about covers the average actual cost of a medical prescription.

In Wales, 74.2 million prescriptions were issued last year costing the Welsh Government the sum of £587 million. What a lot of money could be saved by the WG if the charges for medicines were passed on to the people that actually use them!

There is, however, a history of being generous in Wales, particularly since the Welsh Valleys progeny Aneurin Bevan set up the NHS in the UK shortly after the Second World War, and it is perfectly understandable for modern-day Welsh Labour politicians to want to emulate his generosity by handing out free medicines to everyone. In fact, when prescription charges were first introduced several decades ago, it was generally felt in Wales that this was a form of sacrilege against Aneurin Bevan's fundamental socialist principles. However, times have changed dramatically in the meantime, and we now live in a different kind of culture. Expectations have increased dramatically, and the NHS now has to finance much more expensive equipment and sophisticated techniques, with the result that a basic health service is no longer good enough, and people expect the very best and most advanced treatment as part of their "God-given" entitlement.

People need to realise clearly that there is a financial cost to their treatment, and that medicines are one of the expenses that have to be paid for in some way. In a situation where there is great reluctance to increase taxes and national insurance contributions, it is therefore necessary to find some other means of funding the cost of medicines. This is, of course, most directly achievable via the reintroduction of prescription charges.

If the WG did decide to do this, the charges should not be as excessive as they were in the past, or are in England, but just moderate amounts of perhaps £1 or £2 per prescription. A "back-of-an-envelope" calculation shows that a prescription charge of just £2 would generate an income of approximately £80 million per annum for the WG. This is based on 55% of prescriptions being paid for, while 45% would be exempt from payment. Clearly, it would be harsh and socially unacceptable to charge the under 18's (20% of the population), over 65's (16%) and benefit claimants of working age (9%).

There is a further advantage to this policy. It would also contain an educative element, since patients do need to realise clearly that the medicines they receive from the NHS cost real money, and do not "grow on trees". Since prescription charges were abolished in Wales, the number of prescriptions issued by doctors has increased by 20%. Reintroducing a charge would surely lead to patients taking their medicines more seriously: they would be more inclined to complete their course of treatment, and less inclined to throw them in the wastebin. Apparently, almost 50% of medicines are discarded before the course of treatment is completed. Thus, apart from providing revenue, prescription charges would also reduce wastefulness, possibly improve overall health, and save money that way too.

The Conservative opposition in the Welsh Assembly are already saying that prescription charges should be reintroduced, and that the money saved should be spent on improving other parts of the NHS, such as access to cancer treatments, extra cash for the hospice movement and improvements in stroke care. The Labour leadership in the Welsh Assembly, however, will require a lot of persuasion if they are to change their minds about prescription charges. At present, probably the best ways to influence these policymakers would be to write them a personal letter outlining your views, join in with public debates, and have your say in consultation processes often posted on government or council websites.

Apart from free medical prescriptions, we enjoy the benefits of all sorts of additional aids and services provided by the NHS. For example, patients receive many different types of free surgical appliances, including shoes and surgical boots. (No, I am not going to suggest that people should pay the full price for these!) However, the NHS is definitely exceeding its European legal requirements by providing all the "freebees" it does.

The NHS is the official body providing health care in the UK, and therefore has certain statutory responsibilities. In other countries which do not have a similar public healthcare service, it may be quasi-private insurance companies that organise the basic health care. In Germany, for example, the AOK (Allgemeine Ortskrankenkasse) is responsible. If a patient is prescribed a pair of surgical boots there, for example, this does not come "on the house", but is accompanied by a fixed charge which runs at approximately the average cost of a pair of ordinary non-surgical shoes. In that way the patient is neither cosetted nor penalised for being disabled. He or she simply has to pay the normal and fair price for a pair of shoes, where of course the surgical boots would have cost in practice a great deal more to make, since they have to be custom-made. We could learn a great deal in this country from that attitude. Obviously, nominal charges like this could provide some considerable revenue for the health service in the UK too.

Arguing against this policy, you could say that disabled people already have enough problems and disadvantages to combat, so why make them pay for surgical necessities as well, when they are probably not able to afford them. However, I believe that is an outmoded viewpoint, since – as a result of modern adaptations to working environments, enlightened attitudes and equality laws – many disabled people are actively in work. Those who are not wage earners should, of course, continue not have to pay anything towards their surgical appliances.

Furthermore, it has been standard practice for many years in some countries to levy a nominal "surgery charge". For example, at surgeries in Germany this amounts to 10 Euros (approx. £8) per calender quarter.[11] If you do not need to visit a surgery in a calendar quarter, then you do not pay the charge. Again, this encourages the attitude that it costs money and resources to provide a health centre with doctors, nurses and administrative staff, but it will not unduly punish each patient. No doubt it could be arranged for certain persons on benefits, young children, the old and the disabled to be exempt from such charges.

As mentioned above, the NHS exceeds its remit in many ways. This is probably a reason why so many people enter the UK as "health tourists". We simply have too generous a system. Entitlement to free NHS healthcare seems to be based entirely on residency here, not on whether one pays National Insurance contributions. Although I think the Government is currently trying to tighten up on the rules, I have little confidence that they will get it right.

Car-parking charges

In an ideal world perhaps we would all be able to park our cars free in any town car park. However, the world wouldn't remain ideal for long: within a short time the car park would become full with cars parked and abandoned there all day and every day. For example, some residents and councillors in Usk, Monmouthshire, have fought successfully to keep the town's car parks free (whereas

---

[11] Recently this surgery charge has been dropped in Germany

for most car parks in the county a charge is levied). This has meant that it is often quite difficult for a casual visitor to find a parking space. Some people use the central car park as a place to leave their vehicle all day while they car-share to work in Cardiff, Newport or Bristol. So, simply from the point of view of availability of car-parking spaces for shoppers and visitors, it would be a good idea to charge for parking, so that spaces would be freed-up on a regular basis.

The best compromise I have encountered is where parking for the first hour is entirely free, then an hourly fee is charged after that. In today's world of electronic cards, a barrier at the entrance to the car park would lift on insertion and removal of a debit or credit card, which records the time and details. On leaving the car park, the driver would insert and remove the same card, the appropriate fee would be electronically deducted from the relevant bank account, and the barrier would open.

Of course, this chapter is about obtaining revenue through local charges, and we should certainly not forget that car-parking charges provide a very valuable source of income for councils. In this climate of government cuts, local councils are being faced with increasing pressure from above to axe public services, and councils like Monmouthshire County Council have been agonising over what public services should be withdrawn. In the case of Usk, its library has been earmarked "for the chop", which would make an estimated saving of £330,000 per annum. But why not charge for parking in Usk, I hear a little voice say? That would solve the problem outright. The extra revenue from car park charges would easily pay to keep their beloved library open. County Councillors, please take heed of what I am saying!

Furthermore, when car-parking charges were abolished at Welsh hospitals a few years ago, the WG made another silly vote-catching "give away". I am suggesting that car parking at hospitals should be charged, as in England, but only with a nominal fee of around £1 per day – nothing as extreme as at English hospitals, where it may cost £2 for the first hour of parking, and £1 per hour thereafter (example of charge at Solihull Hospital). This revenue would clearly be useful to offset the cost of providing the car-parking spaces and the salaries of the staff employed there, as well as encouraging mobile patients and visitors to use public transport, so that traffic congestion at hospitals is kept to a minimum.

Conclusion

From the anecdotal examples given above - and there are many more that could be illustrated - the Welsh Government is not providing the right conditions for the NHS to be run in a business-like and efficient manner. By implementing the four simples measures I have outlined above (three of which have no bearing on the actual healthcare itself), the NHS in Wales would probably be able to balance its books without any deterioration in the service, and with no reduction in jobs. The deficit could be paid for by the people who use the service, without punishing anyone unduly, and without having to raise taxes or national insurance contributions.

Chapter 6: REDUCING THE DEFICIT THROUGH INCREASED TAXATION

"The difference between tax avoidance and tax evasion is the thickness of a prison wall." - former Chancellor of the Exchequer, Denis Healey

Preamble

Taxation is a vexing issue for most people. No-one really wants to pay tax, but people are quite vociferous about their right to a high standard of services and benefits, which must of course be paid for somehow. In fact, a large proportion of government spending is on social benefits and the welfare state, which are essentially financed by taxes. The list on the next page shows how total UK government spending is broken down into the various departments.

The public finances are dominated by the welfare state, which cost £203 billion in 2010-11. This includes pensions and tax credits, plus unemployment, sickness, housing, council tax, child support and other benefits. After health and education the biggest drain on the budget is the cost of paying off the interest on the national debt. In 2010-11 these payments reached about £42 billion, more than the entire cost of running the armed forces and about a quarter of the entire deficit. For a healthy budget the total government spending - estimated at £702 billion for the present tax year - should be recooped from tax revenue. However, there is a short-fall of the order of £120 billion.

Should taxes be increased?

The question one might ask then is whether the budget deficit could be eliminated simply by a general increase in income tax. Unfortunately, the answer is 'No'! The deficit is so large, approximately £3,000 per year per capita, that the basic rate of income tax would need to be roughly doubled from 20 to 40% to cover the gap – which gives us a good idea of the scale of the problem. Clearly, an income tax increase of this magnitude would be very unpopular! Politicians in general would never agree to it, nor the wealthy, nor the trade unions, nor the less well off. In fact, most people would reject the idea, even though that is the sort of medicine the country perhaps needs.

UK Government spending (in £ billion)

year	(2010 – 2011)	(2009 – 2010)
Benefits and pensions	202.6	195.5
Health	104.0	99.9
Education	69.2	66.4
Debt interest	42.9	27.2
Defence	36.7	38.7
Local government	30.8	30.1
Scotland	26.1	25.4
Law and Order	19.6	19.6
Wales	14.0	13.6
Northern Ireland	9.9	9.6
EU contributions	7.9	5.6
Transport	6.4	6.4
International aid	6.2	5.5
Other departments	125.4	127.9
Total government spending	701.7	671.4

Far from income tax being increased, we now have the Deputy Prime Minister, Nick Clegg, calling for the personal allowance before paying income tax to be raised, so that each individual would earn more than £10,000 per annum before paying any income tax. This "give-away" would reduce the Exchequer's revenue by approximately £1 billion a year. Mr Clegg wants to finance this preferably by increasing taxes on the rich, but this is unlikely to be agreed to by the Conservative side of the Coalition. The suggestion by Mr Clegg is a good one in principle in that it would help to reduce the inequality of disposable income in the country, a topic that will be discussed in Chapter 10.

I should mention that, at present, tax revenues in the UK add up to 36% of GDP, which is 4% less than the average in the European Union. In other words, UK taxpayers are paying less tax than their European counterparts. Having looked at the deficit figures, and understood the immensity of the problem, I would personally be in favour of a temporary income tax increase that would help to reduce the deficit in the short-term. Unfortunately, many people are so self-centred that, even though they understand that the deficit needs to be reduced or eliminated, they imagine it is up to someone else to make the necessary sacrifices – not themselves!

Conservatives are by definition opposed to high taxation, especially to taxation that affects higher earners. For example, in his March 2012 budget Mr Osborne reduced the top tax band from 50% to 45%, with the excuse that it was not effective enough in producing extra revenue for the Treasury. However, since the deficit is not decreasing as quickly as necessary, he has recently announced that "*the richest will have to pay their fair share...more than they pay at the moment,*" indicating that taxes for the wealthy will have to rise at some point in the future.

The same deficit problem is occurring currently in the USA, and interestingly, in an article to the New York Times, the billionaire investor and philanthropist Warren Buffet has called for Congress to make him and his "mega-rich friends" pay more income tax. He said the rich should do more to plug the deficit. Simultaneously, on this side of the Atlantic, a group comprising some of the richest people in France have offered to sacrifice some of their wealth in a gesture of solidarity, provided it goes towards reducing their country's deficit. An extra 3% of tax has now been announced in France on salaries over 500,000 Euros.

I would certainly suggest that the rich have been cossetted too much, not only in the USA and France but also in the UK, and that they could make a huge positive contribution to freeing their respective countries from some of their deficit. Of course, to be fair, many of the mega-rich are great philanthropists, and do an enormous amount of good, often behind the scenes and out of the media spotlight. Nevertheless, there are a lot of people who have more money than sense, who spend their wealth on senseless and superficial pursuits, when they could be making a positive contribution to the well-being of society. All I can say to them is that it is much more rewarding in life being benevolent than it is being selfish.

The government increased the rate of VAT from 17.5 to 20% at the beginning of 2011, a move that brings in annually several billion pounds extra revenue for the Treasury. After income tax and national insurance contributions, VAT is the third largest source of revenue for the Treasury, but it is disturbing to learn that, as a result of fraud, the UK government has been losing out on as much as 17% of the VAT that it could be collecting. The European Commission has been looking at avoidance of VAT across the EU to help it crack down on this form of criminality. Analysis commissioned from the London consultancy *Reckon* found that Britain had the biggest shortfall in absolute terms of any country in the EU, a figure estimated to be between £13 billion and £18 billion in the year 2006 alone. The report showed that the percentage of VAT lost to fraud in Greece was about 30%, while the figures for Luxembourg, the Netherlands, Sweden and Spain were under 5% of their potential revenue from VAT.[12] Clearly, tax evasion is one of the reasons why Greece has such a large budget deficit, despite efforts by the government to raise enough revenue. Finally, in many countries in northern Europe, VAT is set at a rate of 25%, so there is still considerable room for manouver by the UK government!

---

[12] http://news.bbc.co.uk/1/hi/8335164.stm "Britain losing billions in VAT" by Douglas Fraser

France as an example

The recently elected Socialist government in France under the leadership of Francois Hollande intends to reduce the French budget deficit by means of increased income tax, in preference to government cuts. The policy is to tax high earners (over 1 million euros per annum) at a rate of 75%. However, this has just been scuppered temporarily in the French Constitutional Court, since it appears unfair with regard to the principle of equality. For example, it was pointed out that a household with 2 earners receiving, say, 900,000 euros each – and an income of 1.8 million euros – would pay no tax at the highest rate, whereas a household with only one earner receiving more than 1 million euros, would be taxed at the highest rate. Clearly, the rich will do anything to put a "spanner in the works" of high taxation proposals. However, the court emphatically did not say that the 75% tax rate was too high. The issue on which the government's measure came unstuck was a technicality. In French jargon the new tax bracket for people earning more than a million euros had not been "conjugalised". As framed, the tax band applied to individuals, not to households, but in France, income tax is levied on households. Therefore, the provision breached the constitutional requirement that it be equitable for all. All the government has to do now is reframe and resubmit the proposal.

Tax avoidance and evasion

The Chancellor, Mr Osborne, has been quite adamant and dynamic recently about his desire to fight both tax evasion (illegal) and avoidance (legal). For this purpose he has allocated £900 million to Her Majesty's Revenue and Customs. He has called tax evasion "*morally repugnant... It's stealing from law-abiding people, who face higher taxes to make good the lost revenue. Those who evade taxes, like benefit cheats, are leeches on society. And my message to those who try to hide their incomes from the Revenue in offshore bank accounts and false declarations is simple: we will find you and your money.*"

WAR ON DEBT

Some of the measures that have been unfolded are, as follows. An agreement has now been reached with Switzerland to make it much harder to hide money in Swiss bank accounts. As a result, a "hefty tax" will be imposed on bank accounts held by Britons, and the money passed to the Treasury by the Swiss government, which could potentially bring in billions of pounds in revenue. Mr Osborne said about this: "*It amazes me to hear that the last Labour government had the opportunity to do this a decade ago, but didn't. Just think of the billions of pounds that could have been collected and were instead left in the pockets of the tax cheats. So much for all their talk of fairness. The Swiss tax deal is just the start. We're looking to do more and increase international pressure on those that refuse to co-operate. The number of places to hide money away from the taxman will get smaller and smaller. Tax evaders also make use of tax loopholes, and the truth is that over the last decade they have multiplied. It's up to me as Chancellor to close the loopholes down...And we have taken specific steps to shut down specific avoidance schemes, such as stamp duty and disguised remuneration, which the opposition amazingly voted against in parliament. In total, the tax avoidance measures in this year's budget will raise £1 billion a year... We've also dealt with one of the biggest sources of abuse that we inherited from the last government: the capital gains tax system. We want to encourage genuine enterprise and risk-taking. Instead we found a regime where some of the richest people boasted about paying less tax than their cleaners, by shifting their income into capital gains. That was clearly unfair, and it was costing the taxpayer over £1 billion each year. So we stopped it. Another area where we've taken action is the taxation of non-domiciles. We want Britain to attract talented people from around the world, but it's also right to ask them to make a contribution. Back in 1994 Gordon Brown promised to abolish the non-domicile tax break, but nothing happened and the abuses grew. That's why I proposed as shadow chancellor that wealthy non-doms pay an annual levy for their privileged status, and in the most recent budget I increased the levy to £50,000 a year for those who have lived in Britain for more than 12 years. The record speaks for itself. The last government*

47

presided over a bonanza of tax evasion and avoidance. With this coalition government the hiding places for tax cheats are systematically being shut down. We will make sure that everyone pays their fair share."

Bravo, Mr Osborne, and I hope your plans work in practice! But, however determined those words may sound, I am afraid the financial world will find ways around his measures, for this is just one aspect of the very serious, major global problem of tax havens, as has been dramatically described in Nicholas Shaxson's recent book, *Treasure Islands*.[13]

The Starbucks-type fiddle, or transfer pricing

It is quite interesting to take a specific example of how large American companies manage to avoid paying their fair share of corporation tax in the UK. The campaign organisation *UK Uncut* has recently uncovered the wily dealings of the firm Starbucks, which is one of the largest coffee chains in the UK, and the second largest café or restaurant chain in the world after McDonald's; yet in the last three years they have paid no UK corporation tax at all, despite making sales of £1.2 billion here. Over the last 14 years they have only paid £8.6 million in corporation tax.

In essence, Starbucks have managed to pay no taxes by shifting money around between Starbucks companies in different countries, so that its accounts show it made a loss in the UK. Because of the way they did this inside their global corporate empire, no one knows exactly how much tax Starbucks should have paid. Comparing Starbucks to other similar US based multinationals, McDonald's had a tax bill of over £80 million on £3.6 billion of UK sales. Kentucky Fried Chicken, incurred taxes of £36 million on £1.1 billion pounds in UK sales.

According to *UK Uncut* there are three ways Starbucks managed to move their money out of the UK so they could dodge corporation tax. Firstly, they used the fact that brand names are worth money, and businesses can pay money to the part of their

---

[13] *Treasure Islands: Tax Havens and the Men who Stole the World* by Nicholas Shaxson, Vintage Press, 2011

business that owns the brand for the privilege of using it. In the UK, Starbucks paid 6% of its total sales as a 'royalty' to Starbucks in Amsterdam – taking plenty of profit out of the UK to the Netherlands where they have a secret low-rate tax deal with the Dutch government. Secondly, although Switzerland is not a coffee-growing country, this is where it gets its coffee beans from. It appears Starbucks is buying very, very expensive coffee beans from its own subsidiary in Switzerland, where commodities like coffee are taxed at only 5%, compared to paying 24% corporation tax in the UK. Thirdly, in the UK companies can deduct the interest they pay on loans from their taxable income, so the UK company borrows money from another Starbucks subsidiary in a tax haven where interest payments aren't taxed. Starbucks' entire UK operation is funded by debt, and very expensive debt at that, which is a very bad deal for the UK subsidiary, but a very good deal for the Starbucks company lending the money.

If one looks into it, one finds that this is the standard and very common way for multi-national companies to minimise their tax payments. It is definitely immoral, even if it might not be strictly illegal. Nicholas Shaxson[13] does suggest how governments could try to make multi-nationals liable for tax fairly, and this would involve firstly knowing the total global profit of the company in question, including all its subsidiaries. A formula then specifies what proportion of the activities of the company occurs in each country. This could be determined from the payroll in that country, for example, in some internationally agreed way. Next the profit is apportioned to each country, and then each government taxes that fractional profit at the respective rate applicable to all its resident companies. Easy! Now make it work!

Conclusion

On the one hand, people have increasing expectations when it comes to health care, education, policing, road maintenance and social services, etc.; on the other hand, they do not seem to realise adequately that – if we want to maintain these public services – it costs a great deal of money. Taxation now needs to increase to cover the escalating costs. The skill required of the Chancellor now is to be able to balance income tax levels in such a way that they appear reasonable, and to close loopholes and tax dodges that allow wealthy individuals and multi-national corporations to avoid paying their fair amount of UK tax.

Chapter 7: PRIVATISATION OF PUBLIC ASSETS

"First of all the Georgian silver goes, and then all that nice furniture that used to be in the salon. Then the Canalettos go." - Harold Macmillan (on privatisation), speech to the Tory Reform Group, November 1985

Preamble

We have so far discussed government cuts, income generation and tax increases as methods of solving the deficit problem, but there is another way the government can obtain revenue, via privatisation, which will be debated in the present chapter.

Privatisation of public assets as an ideological principle

First let me quote a few sentences from a report issued by the Organisation for Economic Cooperation and Development (Source: Privatising State-Owned Enterprises, OECD, 2003):
"*By the 1970s, the poor performance of state-owned companies was acknowledged and various efforts were made to improve performance. However, over time, effectiveness of such efforts and the sustainability of the results achieved were questioned and, as a consequence, by the middle of the 1980s and particularly in the 1990s the policy debate focussed on the issue of state-ownership itself, and whether it mattered. By the 1990s privatisation had become a key component of economic reform throughout the OECD area....One of the most important policy objectives of privatisation is to improve the efficiency and performance of companies. Despite the difficulties with data and methodology, there is overwhelming support for the notion that privatisation brings about a significant increase in the profitability, real output and efficiency of privatised companies.*"

The above paragraph, to be found in an important OECD document, is clearly pretty damning of state-run companies, and music in the ears of free-market capitalists. But is it necessarily true? It is most definitely a matter of opinion, I would say. One of the most significant clauses in the above paragraph, that one could easily gloss over, is *"Despite the difficulties with data and methodology..."* In my view, this is an astonishingly poor remark to make in such an important document: it essentially means that the OECD is admitting they have no proper scientific proof that privatisation is any better than public ownership! In other words, what we have read above is more like "hearsay" than "fact". Nevertheless, right or wrong, this "privatisation religion" has influenced the mindset of economists and politicians in many countries for at least the past thirty years.

The drive to privatise British industry

The sale of British Telecom in 1984 is considered to be the harbinger of the launch of large-scale privatisations that were begun in the UK by Mrs Thatcher's government in the 1980s. The privatisation drive during this period was fuelled by the following factors, in particular, an ideological antipathy for the state playing a large rôle in the economy, disillusion with the general inefficiency of state-owned enterprises, and a desire to combat the excessive power of the trade unions. Added to this was the trend to liberalisation and globalisation of financial markets, and possibly one could argue that technological changes in sectors such as telecommunications and electricity generation had made monopolies in the provision of certain goods and services obsolete. In addition, privatisation is used as a source of revenue for the Treasury.

Privatisation has generally been accompanied by restructuring of each company prior to the sell-off, and coupled with this by job losses. Employment losses tend to be largest where the industry faces excess capacity, and technological changes increase competition without increasing demand, whereas in sectors such as telecommunications, where market liberalisation and growing demand for new services create new employment opportunities, the net job losses tend to be smaller.

Privatisation proceeds are raised through offering shares on the stock market, but the policy on foreign ownership of privatised state-owned enterprises can be a sensitive issue, particularly in the context of industries that are considered to be of national and strategic importance. In the UK, the policy has been one of openness to foreign investment in privatised companies. In France, prior to 1996, the initial privatisation law of 1986 set a maximum ceiling on share ownership by non-EU investors at around 20% of the total share capital of a privatised company. However, since 1996 those restrictions have been removed. The view of the OECD is that it is more efficient to remove all restrictions to foreign ownership, in order to maximise the capital gained on sale. This open policy has resulted in most of Britain's utilities now being owned by foreign companies, over which we do not have the control we once had.

Governments succeeding Mrs Thatcher's have hardly altered their thinking on this issue. For example, the present government has recently sold the rights for running the Channel Tunnel Rail Link to a Canadian consortium for a sum of several billion pounds. Mr Cable's department did, however, point out that this was on a 25 year lease, and that subsequently the company would revert to the public sector. This is clearly better than selling the company off completely. The question that never seems to be asked is: if a foreign company can run a British business at a profit – and that is obviously their aim – then why can't the UK government do this on behalf of the taxpayer - "at arms length", as one often says? The profits would then go towards balancing the budget, of course. The government has just announced it also intends to sell our 40% stake in the cross-channel express rail service Eurostar.

The opposite to privatisation occurred recently when, due to the insolvency of many banks, many of them were brought under government control. However, the government is now intent on re-privatising these banks, a move that would at least recoup some of the taxpayers' money that was used in the bail-outs.

Nick Clegg, realising that the public felt they wanted something back from the bank bail-outs, recently suggested giving these banks away in the form of free shares to each member of the general public. Surely, in the light of the huge budget deficit and national debt, free government give-aways must be totally out of the question? The best long-term policy must surely be to keep the bailed-out banks nationalised, so that the public can benefit from their profits in the long run.

It is still very worrying to contemplate what national assets the government might still decide to sell-off, in order to obtain a "quick fix" to some of the deficit problem. Someone joked recently that Greece should sell a few of its islands to pay off its debts. Twenty to thirty years ago Mrs Thatcher actually sold-off our reservoirs, the tele-communications industry, power stations, airports, etc., comprising unimaginable amounts of land and real estate in the UK belonging to the general public. In the meantime, much of Britain's defence industry has also been privatised, as well as the steel industry, and much more that I have not mentioned here. This has been, in my opinion, one of the most short-sighted and damaging things that has ever been done to this country.

To cap it all, the present coalition government has just privatised the Royal Mail, including Parcelforce, completely against the wishes of almost everyone in the country. The majority of the workers themselves are also against the idea, but – as often happens – the workforce have been bribed into going along with it. The bribery comes in the form of free shares. Each full-time member of staff received 725 shares, which are valued at £3,545, with the stipulation that they are not allowed to be sold for three years. Excuse me, but that is our money you (the Government) are giving away!

On their first day of trading of the floated company, the shares were selling at 475p each, which is 44% higher than the issue price of 330p. This clearly suggests that Royal Mail was undersold by approximately £1 billion. Critics warn there is no protection against the company falling into foreign hands and there is no guarantee that post offices especially in rural areas will now be able to stay open. The Business Secretary, Vince Cable, has pushed through the sale of Royal Mail, claiming that it "*had to be done*". Ironically, even Margaret Thatcher drew the line at privatising the Royal Mail.

To avoid any confusion, I should mention that Post Office Ltd is a separate company from Royal Mail, and will not be privatised. This is a retail company that provides a wide range of products including postage stamps and banking to the public through its nationwide network of post office branches. Fortunately this company will for the foreseeable future remain owned by the UK government.

The unexpected consequences of privatisation

When Thatcher carried through her privatisation plan in the 1980s and sold off the UK's publicly-owned corporations, she probably did not envisage what far-reaching negative consequences her policy would eventually have. The privatisation was implemented against what were portrayed by Conservatives to be outdated and inefficient, socialist monolithic institutions – the nationalised industries - and also aimed at silencing the militant trade unions, as I have already mentioned. There were further reasons: the revenue from the sales was very useful for the Exchequer, enabling the Conservatives to keep taxes lower than they would otherwise have been (remembering that low taxes are popular with the electorate and would gain votes). Furthermore, with the creation of lots of small shareholders, the British electorate would be transformed into a nation of "petty capitalists" who were most likely to vote Tory at the next election. In addition, privatisation was an admirable opportunity for various private investors and financiers to make huge personal gains from the sales.

To return to the consequences of the privatisation exercise, over the next twenty years or so most of these companies subsequently became owned not by the bourgeoisie of "Middle England" as Mrs Thatcher would presumably have hoped, but by foreign investors. Most of the utilities, such as the gas, electricity and water boards, soon became part of large French or German agglomerates, such as EDF and E.ON. The British Steel Corporation, as British Steel, was soon taken over by the Dutch firm Hoogovens, transformed into a much slimmer Corus, and then recently purchased by the Indian company Tata. I'm not saying it is wholly bad for companies to be foreign-owned, because foreign ownership has certainly brought with it expertise, and achieved what seems to be a real improvement in efficiency. I am merely saying that too many of these companies are foreign-owned.

This applies not just to the former nationalised industries but also to countless private companies. For example, Spanish companies have recently bought the British mobile phone operator O2, the Abbey Banking Group, and the British Airports Authority (BAA), which owns and runs most of the UK's airports including Heathrow. The French, meanwhile, have acquired defence businesses such as Shorts Missile Systems and Racal Electronics. A couple of years ago, the hugely important shipping company P&O was bought by Dubai Ports, and recently Imperial Chemical Industries was aquired by its Dutch rival, Akzo. The list goes on and on *ad nauseam*, but - if nothing changes soon - I suppose the aquisitions will eventually inevitably dry up when all significant British companies have finally been taken over.

Foreign companies wishing to acquire British businesses have actually been encouraged to do so. For example, when he was Prime Minister, Tony Blair ruled out any possibility that the government would block a bid by Gazprom, the state-run Russian gas company, when it expressed interest in buying the privatised British energy group, Centrica (the company owning British Gas). The former prime minister even spoke out against "economic patriotism", as though it were a dirty word. However, no other country in the industrialised world would be foolish enough to allow its strategic assets to be bought up in such a short-sighted way.

There are countless logical reasons why it is sensible for home industries to be locally owned, without being protectionist. For example, when times are hard, foreign owners will be less willing to invest in British subsidiaries and may be tempted to close them. This happened recently to the L'Oreal factory near Cardiff. The Tata-owned Llanwern steelworks, near my home town, also does not seem to have a future, with the loss of a considerable number of skilled jobs.

Furthermore, the aluminium works owned by the Indian company Novelis at Rogerstone, near Newport in South Wales recently closed putting 450 people out of work; the Italian-owned Hoover factory in Merthyr Tydfil producing washing-machines closed for production putting about 340 people out of work, and the Italian company Indesit that fairly recently bought the British washing-machine manufacturing company Hotpoint in Denbighshire North Wales also closed with the loss of 305 jobs. The Hotpoint factory in Peterborough making fridges was closed by Indesit in 2007. The result is that if you now go to a retailer to buy, e.g., a refrigerator, washing machine, or virtually any white-goods product, you will almost certainly find that the vast majority are manufactured in China. They may even have an English-sounding brand name such as Fridgemaster, Whirlpool, Electrolux or Hotpoint stuck on the front – a clever ploy to make you think you are buying British.

Many such companies were once upon a time respected and successful British-owned businesses. Every time a UK manufacturing company ceases operation, apart from the social deprivation caused by people losing their jobs in a single place in one fell swoop, the taxpayer has to "pick up the pieces" and pay for the additional unemployment and social welfare benefits. On top of that, however, there is an additional cost to the country as a whole, since goods that are no longer produced locally will have to be imported, thus contributing to a further increase in the already horrendously large balance of payments deficit. This will be discussed in Chapter 8.

There is also insidious long-term harm done to the country, as expressed, for example, by Gordon Campbell, chairman of Babcock International who, concerned with know-how, skills, techniques, software and business processes, said: "*The perceived wisdom is that ownership doesn't matter, but I don't think that is the case. The acquirer tends to suck in the intellectual property to wherever its headquarters is based. That denudes Britain, undermining the long-term viability of British industry.*"

Evidence has also been accumulating recently that Spanish companies have been advantaged by their own tax rules when bidding for British companies, which enabled them to underbid British companies. In addition, there is concern that the Spanish company, Ferrovial, which bought BAA, will not be able to afford to carry out the required improvements at Heathrow Airport in future which are needed to maintain London's position as a major hub of financial activity.

There is no doubt that some companies are of crucial national strategic importance, and it is obvious that such assets should remain in British hands. The government should surely compile a list of "companies not for sale." My list would start with defence procurement, then the utilities (gas, electricity, water), telecommunications, oil, steel, coal, aerospace, airports and ports. Apart from that, I would like the government to ensure that in each branch of industry the UK has at least one UK-owned manufacturing company producing aircraft, cars, lorries, buses, televisions, electrical white goods, computers, mobile phones, etc., so that the British public at least have the option of being able to use or purchase each item they require from a UK-owned company manufacturing in the UK. This is not something unreasonable I am suggesting. In fact, it is only what most large industrialised nations are already trying to do.

Conclusion

The pros and cons of privatisation versus public ownership are tainted with acrimonious and prejudiced allegations, even amongst experts, such as those at the OECD. The sell-off of Britain's utilities, started by Mrs Thatcher in the 1980s, has had massively undesirable effects, resulting in a huge increase in foreign ownership. Meanwhile, most of our manufacturing industry has capitulated and closed down, with the result that imports are at a record high. The only way of recovering now is for the government to focus its attention on providing a platform for strategic state manufacturing of most of our consumer goods that are presently made in China, other parts of Asia and Germany. Allowing private enterprise to dictate the way our economy operates will never result in the correct balance or amount of production.

Chapter 8: BRITAIN'S BALANCE OF PAYMENTS

"The drain on Britain's gold reserves has finally come to an end. They've all gone." - David Frost, That Was the Week That Was, BBC Television (1963)

Preamble

At the heart of Britain's economic woes, including its debt problem, lies the country's serious imbalance in trade between exports and imports. For the past sixteen years, coinciding with when New Labour first came to power, Britain's trade deficit in goods has been deteriorating rapidly. The issue seems almost to have been ignored publicly. The trade gap in goods is now historically at its worst ever level. The details make for disturbing reading.

UK imports and exports

The next figure shows in money terms how Britain's total exports and imports in goods and services have changed between 1947 and 2007. The graphs are derived from tables of data published by the Office for National Statistics (ONS), and corrected for inflation to 2007 prices according to the official Pound Deflator (which I shall explain below).

The data seem to indicate that foreign trade has expanded by a factor of eight over the years since WW2, from £50 billion in the year 1947 to about £400 billion in 2007. However, although globalisation has led to a marked increase in world trade since WW2, I do not believe there has been as great an increase in volume as suggested by the official data. I suggest that the way the current money values have been adjusted for inflation using the GDP pound deflator does not give a true picture; the deflator (just like the Consumer Price Index CPI) has been underestimating the devaluation of the pound over many decades (see also Chapter 11).

Figure 8.1: UK import and export trade in goods and services (corrected for inflation)[14]

Britain's trade balance

The absolute values of imports and exports shown above are clearly of huge importance, but it is the difference between them that constitutes the balance of payments – and this gives us an indication of how much poorer or richer the country is becoming. It's like the country's capital income and expenditure balance sheet: if you sell more than you buy, you make a profit, but if you buy in more than you sell, then you have a deficit. This is the situation at present. We are importing far more than we are exporting, and this has to be paid for somehow – so we have to sell our assets, or take out credit and get into debt. In the next graph I

---

[14] Source: National Statistics website: www.statistics.gov.uk

have plotted the trade balance from 1945 to 2012 corrected for inflation according to the pound deflator.

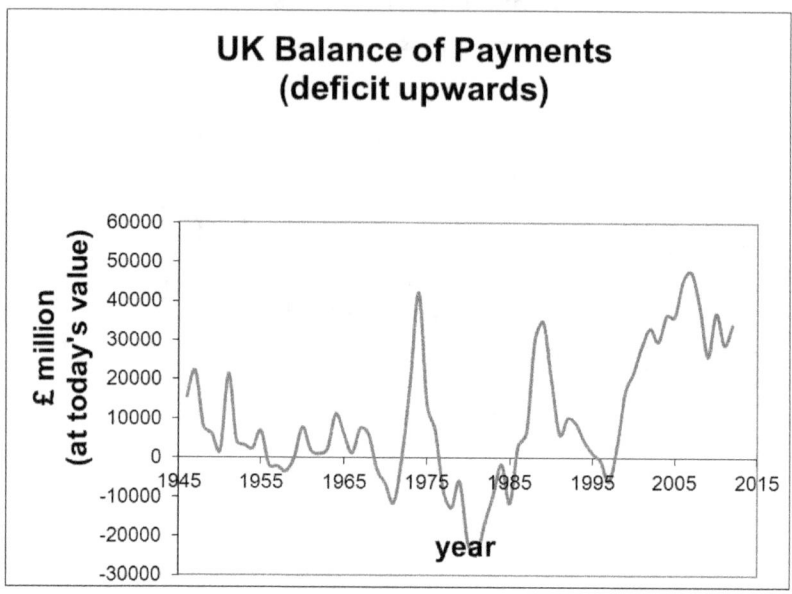

Fig. 8.2:   *Britain's Balance of Payments (goods and services)*

Reading from the left of the graph: the first peak reflects the economic difficulties encountered in rebuilding the country immediately after WW2. The peaks in the 1950s relate, amongst other things, to the costs of the Korean War and the Suez Crisis. A surplus occurred towards the end of the 1960s, as a result of Harold Wilson's strategy of trying to stop money flowing out of the country. (Remember, when each person was only allowed to take £50 of foreign currency when going on a continental holiday?)

The huge deficit spike in 1974 coincides with the events surrounding industrial unrest, strikes and Edward Heath's infamous "Three Day Week". Then there was a large fall in the deficit - even a large surplus - as a result of the bonanza due to North Sea oil. After that, still under Mrs Thatcher, the deficit rose between 1985 and 1990 to very high levels and we started importing goods excessively to fuel the country's insatiable greed for more and more consumer products.

When John Major came to office in 1990 the deficit decreased. This was due, to a large extent, to the deregulation of financial services and the increased success of the City of London in "creaming off" a proportion of the money flowing through the capital. By 1997 there was even a slight surplus.

However, after Tony Blair and New Labour came to power in 1997, under Gordon Brown as Chancellor, the trade deficit began to worsen again. By 2007 it had reached £43 billion. The trade deficit in manufactured goods was actually far, far worse, approaching £90 billion, but this was offset by a trade surplus in services of more than £40 billion. For the past decade or so the trade gap has been consistently running at between 2 to 3% of GDP.

We should again notice that the peaks in the deficit just after WW2 in the previous diagram look relatively small compared to the deficit today. However, many of us know from personal experience that at that time Britain had a very serious crisis with its trade deficit. Thus, we are led to infer that there could be two possible explanations for what appears to be a "skew" in the graph: (i) the trade gap is far worse today than it was just after WW2 when the country was almost bankrupt, and/or (ii) the official inflation figures do not provide a realistic pound deflator for the macroeconomy, resulting in peaks being compressed artificially as we look back in time. I think that both of these explanations are valid to some extent.

It is illuminating to replot data by separating out the trade in goods from the trade in services. In order to obtain a measure for the true size of the trade balance that is independent of the pound deflator, it is usual to express the figures as a percentage of GDP. The next graph shows these quantities over the time period from 1955 to the present. The curve marked 'Total' is the trade balance for all goods and services, where I have now plotted a surplus upwards or a deficit downwards. Over most of the period, there has been a deficit. At present this deficit lies at about 2% of GDP. Although this is not the worst the trade deficit has ever been in terms of GDP, there is a very disturbing feature: if you split the trade into the two major aspects, goods and services, you find an enormous trade deficit in goods of about 7% of GDP, which is offset by a surplus in services of about 5%. This trade deficit in goods, however, is rapidly and inexorably becoming worse every year, a trend which has now lasted for about the past 16 years.

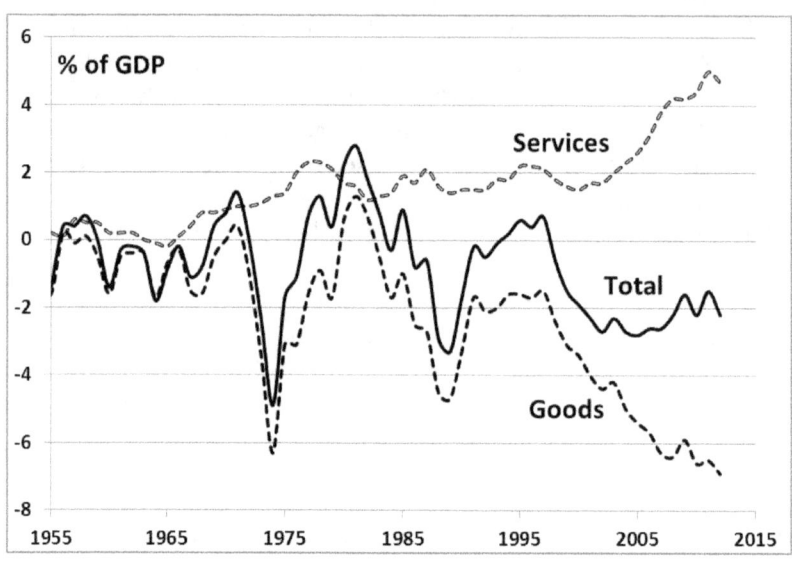

Fig.8.3   *Britain's trade balance in % of GDP since 1955 (N.B. deficit downwards)*

Historically and today

We learn from our history books that the Industrial Revolution began around 1850 - but in the meantime things have changed drastically. Whereas one century ago half the world's coal was mined in the South Wales valleys to fire its industries and navy, today this place where I now live - the "Land of My Fathers" - feels more like an industrial heritage museum. The City of Birmingham, where I was born, used to be the "hub of the world" when it came to manufacturing. However, most of Britains's "old industries" were dismantled during the time of Margaret

Thatcher's government, and this process of decline has continued ever since.

Replacement by newer technologies has occurred to some extent, but Britain's manufacturing sector is now just a very pale shadow or slimmed-down version of its former greatness. Indeed, the entire production sector today makes up only 22% of Britain's output, whereas the service sector is responsible for 78% of it. The table below lists some of the most important branches and their respective GDP (as value added) in 2011:-

Contributions to UK GDP

£ billion

Services

Wholesale and retail trade	151.8
Real estate and renting	143.6
Financial and business services	116.4
Health and social work	104.0
Creative industries	98.0
Education services	84.6
Administration and defence	70.4
Transport and storage	59.2
Hotels and restaurants	36.6
Telecommunications	25.1
Tourism	24.9

Production

Construction industry	86.8
Automotive manufacturing	52.5
Electricity, gas and water supply	33.3
Mining and quarrying	31.4
Aerospace industries	20.0
Agriculture and fisheries	9.4
Pharmaceutical industry	8.4

Currency issues

Britain clearly needs to export more goods, but one of the main problems faced by Britain's manufacturing industry today is that the pound Sterling is overvalued against foreign currencies. Take the euro, for example, which is now trading at about 1.2 euros per pound. Anyone who travels to the continent of Europe where the euro is the national currency will soon realise that you can often obtain equivalent goods there for the same number of euros as you would pay in pounds in the UK. The pound may be overvalued against the euro by possibly up to 20% at present, i.e., parity with the euro would be a more realistic level. This makes exporting British goods to the EU extremely difficult, and the import of foreign goods attractive – which is bad for Britain's own industry and employment. (I should perhaps add that casual tourists do not generally get this impression of the exchange rate, partly because banks give them a very poor exchange rate on the currency they buy, and partly because inexperienced tourists do not generally obtain the best value for money when they are on holiday in tourist resorts.)

The situation with respect to the Chinese currency is even more unbalanced. Since the Chinese do not have such an open economy as in the West, their government is able to manipulate their currency, the Yuan, at an unrealistically low level against the American dollar. This means that the Chinese are able to export phenomenal amounts of goods to the rest of the world, and have now overtaken Germany as the world's largest exporting country. At the same time, they are amassing vast quantities of gold and foreign exchange reserves. The Chinese people themselves are only slowly beginning to benefit from the immense wealth being generated in their country. The situation with respect to China might improve as time goes on, as the Chinese currency gradually begins to establish itself as a global reserve currency (see also Chapter 13).

Wage issues

Linked to the currency issue is the problem of wage costs. For example, the German company BOSCH recently closed a car-parts factory in South Wales with the loss of about 900 jobs. The work will go to Hungary where the wage costs are approximately 65% of those in the UK. Clearly the German company is acting mainly on economic grounds in a very competitive world market. If it has the choice of a factory in Wales or one in Hungary operating with 35% reduced wage costs, it will choose the Hungarian location. There is no need for it to show any loyalty to the UK...or is there? It is certainly a fact that the Welsh Development Agency provided a grant of £21 million to encourage BOSCH in the first place to locate to Wales in 1991 when the factory was opened.

Apart from a reduction in Sterling's exchange rate value, which would lower labour costs compared to Euroland, there seem to me to be two other ways to combat this problem. The first is for companies to invest in measures that will increase productivity, and the second is for the employees to take a reduction in pay. The trade unions involved are not going to regard the latter suggestion favourably at all. It is traditionally out of the question, or so it appears. It seems that unions are prepared to see their members out of work entirely and dependent on government help, rather than for them to accept wage cuts. An example is the recent situation at the Grangemouth refinery. The owners had to actually close down the plant, making all the workers redundant, before the union would agree to wage cuts and other changes. It *is* a fact that Britons are paying themselves too much. But, why should a worker on an assembly line in the North of England or Wales sacrifice a large chunk of his hard-earned, fairly meagre wage, when bankers up in London are still paying themselves massive bonuses?

Global pollution and the carbon footprint

Another related issue of enormous significance is that China is now responsible for 24% of global carbon dioxide emissions, followed by the US with 22%; the entire European Union produces 12%, India 8% and the Russian Federation 6%. One of the reasons China's goods are so inexpensive is that they do not have such strict controls on pollution as we do in Europe. By purchasing cheap manufactured goods from China, we are in effect contributing to the marked increase in global atmospheric pollution. Surely this is a good reason to keep manufacturing locally, where pollution control is better, technology is cleaner, and emissions due to long distance transport of goods are minimised?

Coordinating government policy with manufacturing industry

Since the 1980s until very recently there has been, apparently, almost a complete disregard by governments for the UK's manufacturing industry. It seems as if they are afraid of "getting their hands dirty". There has been a misguided political view that industry will take care of itself and should be left to market factors. If there is a need, then someone in the private sector will somehow come up with the answer.

This free market, "hands-off" attitude, however, could lead to economic suicide. It is certainly simplistic and short-sighted. For a start, the gaps in consumer demand are almost always filled by foreign products: computers, flat-screen televisions, you name it, it will have been made somewhere else - and it does matter intensely for the health of British education, design, research, development, production and employment. For all too long we have been governed by ignoramuses of science, engineering and technology - people unable to see the significance of manufacturing. It is therefore urgently necessary that the state should coordinate its policies with the demands and needs of the 21st century in Britain. State intervention in production is essential. Planning is inevitable. It is a myth that private investment will solve the problems: private investors are mainly interested in making a short-term profit; long-term planning requires government action.

I would like to give a hypothetical example of the kind of thing I mean. We have experienced over many years the rise and fall of the British motor industry. At one time more cars were made in Britain than in any other country in the world. We still have a large number of old-timers lovingly preserved and driven with great pride on special occasions, nearly all of them makes that no longer exist: Riley, Wolseley, Morris, Austin, Hillman, Humber, Triumph, Rover, TVR, and so on. These days most of the makes that are still manufactured are foreign-owned: Jaguar, Land Rover, Mini, Rolls Royce, Bentley, Ford and Vauxhall. It "makes the heart bleed" to think about it too deeply - the next generation of enthusiasts won't have any truly British cars to be proud of at all.

However, the motor industry is essentially an old industry based on a type of vehicle with an inherently inefficient engine operating via the internal combustion of non-renewable fossil fuels, which give off large amounts of toxic emissions and greenhouse gases. In the meantime, in countries like Germany and France vast resources have been invested into technology that makes the motor car today more efficient, but still essentially the same.

I can very well imagine a situation where the government decided it would have to pass a law allowing only zero-emission vehicles into the centres of cities, in order to make them free of pollution and the environment much healthier and much more pleasant. It would probably save the NHS a considerable amount of money in the long run, and immensely improve the quality of life of the general public.

This idea - however splendid it may sound - is not practicable because we haven't as yet developed the technology or production capacity to do it ourselves in Britain. The Japanese have, however, and if it suddenly became law, they would flood our streets with their hybrid and electric vehicles.

The intelligent approach would be for the government, well in advance of any proposed law, to create a publicly owned company that did research, development and ultimately produced the required specification of vehicle. The amount of government investment needed would be "chicken feed" compared to the amounts of money currently being thrown at private banks, for example.[15]

---

[15] In my opinion it is not adequate for the government to use taxpayers' money in

When the time was ripe for introducing the requirement of pollution-free vehicles - up to ten years can elapse between concept stage and production - manufacturing industry would already have in place enough production capacity to meet the demand. It is not good enough just to leave such important issues to the whims of the free market, operating on the principle of short-term financial gain, and to predatory foreign investors.

In Britain today there are miriads of small innovative companies researching into green technologies. However, if the government fails to support these technologies in a major way, including the production end of the process, then the intellectual property and the manufacturing capability will inevitably be bought up and wander out of the country. It is so important that the government involves itself on a large scale to maintain Britain as a manufacturing base, because private enterprise is failing to do this. There are many more examples of where this approach should be implemented, for example, in the fields of renewable energy, medical technology, transport and most certainly military technology.

Conclusion

Britain's balance of payments deficit in goods is historically at its worst level ever. It is completely unsustainable to keep importing vastly more goods than we export. We are only managing to do this at present by excessive borrowing as well as selling off the country's assets. It needs to dawn on the general public as well as the government that we urgently need to return to being a country that manufactures or produces its own wealth.

---

setting up private-public funding initiatives (PFIs) or consortia of mainly foreign firms and British finance institutions to provide the infrastructure that this country desperately needs.

WAR ON DEBT

Chapter 9: PERSONAL DEBT

"Live now, pay later" - film by Jack Trevor Story (1962) taken from Jack Lindsay's novel, "All on the Never-Never"

Preamble

The national debt only represents the government's part of the overall debt. The total public and private debt, i.e., a country's total external liabilities, or external debt, which is ultimately repayable in foreign currency, goods or services, is far greater. The population of this country have taken out huge amounts of personal or private debt which is not included in the public debt figures discussed in Chapter 2, so in this chapter we shall take a brief look at the issue of personal debt.

Personal debt

The average person in the UK appears on the face of it to be better off than ever before. If you look around you, you will see young people driving very expensive cars; they all possess sophisticated electronic equipment, such as iPhones and tablet computers; the homes of even the least well-off people probably contain large-screen televisions, huge refrigerators and expensive furnishings – all indicative of an affluent lifestyle. In itself this is no bad thing, but how many of these wonderful consumer items have actually been paid for? The chances are that many of these people are living off credit. What has been occurring recently – much more than ever before – is that, in order to finance their relatively high standard of living now, they have accrued a great deal of debt that must be paid off in the future.

The total private or personal debt of the individuals and families in the country is made up essentially of mortgages, credit card debt and other personal loans. Mortgages comprise by far the biggest contribution, approximately 90% of the total debt. The *Money Charity's* website[16] gives a snapshot of some of the

71

important data. For instance, in August 2013 the average private debt per household in the UK was £54,141, and the total daily amount of interest paid on personal debt in the country amounted to £164 million. This, of course, has dire consequences for many people: 84 properties are repossessed every day in the UK, on average, and 282 people are declared insolvent or bankrupt. The total outstanding personal debt is approximately £1.427 trillion, of which £1.246 trillion is mortgage debt, the rest being unsecured debt or consumer credit amounting to £159 billion. At present there are about 11.3 million mortgages, with an average outstanding debt of £113,000. The total credit card debt was £57.2 billion in August 2013, with 62.3% of cards being charged interest at rates of the order of 10 to 20%, which is far, far higher than the Bank of England's lending rate.

Why is this very bad?

Debt is very divisive: it divides those who borrow from those who lend. I can just imagine, in a Dickensian sense, money lenders like Uriah Heep in *David Copperfield* rubbing their hands together with glee at the thought of loaning money for profit, while their debtors are desperately struggling just to get by (one of my emotional tirades in this book!).

Personally, I think of *debt* as an enemy, or perhaps a vice, that needs to be eradicated from one's life. It's dirty and filthy, and you don't want to have anything to do with it! This is how I felt about smoking when I tried to give up the awful habit many years ago. As it happens, I found it easy for two reasons: one, I realised it would kill me prematurely if I kept up the habit; two, I did not like to think that I was getting poorer while the tobacco companies and the taxman were getting richer at my expense. Smoking was equivalent to throwing money down the drain. Motivated like that, I had no difficulty at all giving it up. In some ways, being in serious debt is similar. It could kill you prematurely, because it stultifies your life and causes great anxiety or emotional stress; and it also keeps you poor.

---

[16] http://themoneycharity.org.uk/media/Debt-Stats-Full-October-2013.pdf

WAR ON DEBT

Debt is, of course, often triggered by temptation. Just like the smoking temptation: 'Have a fag, Ant. Oh, go on, why not? Just one.' In the car salesroom we might hear, 'Now this is just the right set of wheels for you, Sir. It will satisfy all your requirements! I'll call our finance manager; he can easily arrange a loan for you.' Temptation is with us all the time, but perhaps we need to be clear about it. There is nothing wrong with temptation itself. Do not feel guilty if you sponaneously have the temptation to murder your boss and go off to the Bahamas with his wife! The crucial thing for you is *not* to fall into that trap! Temptation should be regarded as just a challenge enabling you to demonstrate your own strength of character – by resisting it. You will actually be better off afterwards if you do resist it. The same applies to debt. Resist the temptation. Show that *you* are in command of your life.

If debt is so bad for individuals, then why does it occur at all? Personal debt often arises simply through overspending - by purchasing some material good that one really shouldn't purchase at the time. In other words, a major cause of personal debt in our country is not caused by *need*, but by *wanting* too much and too soon. The pressures on young people are particularly strong in this respect. For example, if you don't own the latest iPhone then you are a particularly sad character amongst your peers. Young people represent a massive market that is being exploited mercilessly by unscrupulous commercial sharks. But the vast majority of personal debt in this country is not of this kind: it is housing debt in the form of mortgages, nice respectable mortgages! The issue of mortgage debt will be discussed in more detail in a later chapter.

Unfortunately, debt is not always of one's own making. There are times when fortune seems to work against all your plans and aspirations: you are made redundant, you have an accident, become ill, you are faced with divorce or some other personal tragedy. What do you do then if your outgoings exceed your income? This is when you need help. This is not when you take out a high-interest loan to pay the rent and other bills in the hope that things will soon get better. Our social welfare system *will* keep you from starving and being homeless, if you follow the correct procedures.

But at the end of the day (to use a very hackneyed expression) we are actually all helpless at being able to combat debt, because – as we shall see later - it is intrinsically part and parcel of our capitalist economic system, or more accurately our monetary system. That is the ultimate reason why debt is so insidious (Chapter 13 deals with this).

Creating wealth instead of debt

I expect you are probably a product of the post-war era in western Europe, as I am. Personally, I am very thankful to have lived through the best period ever in the history of mankind, and probably in one of the best places in the entire world – even though I admit to spending quite a lot of my time complaining about the British weather! Due to our current medical knowledge, welfare state and political system, I would not have wanted to live at any other time in history. But, to be honest, I am worried about the future, not for my own sake, but for the sake of the next generation and their children. The problem that is becoming increasingly apparent is that the standard of living we are used to, and automatically expect, is not sustainable. Apart from using up the planet's precious resources at an alarming rate and damaging the earth's ecology and atmosphere, we are also not currently *earning* the affluence and quality of life we have come to expect as our inalienable right. Instead we are *borrowing* our high standard of living.

Many years ago, as a young person, I did not understand this issue. I took everything around me for granted: plentiful food, a house to live in, transport, medical care, school, etc. The world was simply there for me to make the most of in my own selfish way. I did not realise that everything I possessed had been worked and fought for by my predecessors, including my parents. In recent years it has dawned upon me that our affluence and well-being are somewhat fragile, and if I look at many other places in the world, no such affluence and security exists. If I examine my own contribution to society, I concede that I have never done anything significant that would directly add to the wealth of the country. As a teacher, I was essentially providing a service rather than producing anything. Of course, I am nothing unusual. Most people do not *directly* create any wealth for the country.

So, where does our wealth come from? This is a complex question that I shall try to deal with in the book. I think it is important for everyone to ask this sort of question of themselves: What have I done to deserve all that I possess? If you ask yourself a question like this, you may not take so much for granted. You might then realise that affluence has to be worked for, and it has a price. It does not grow on trees. We cannot afford to be complacent in a competitive world. But we also need to share our affluence fairly amongst all people, especially those who cannot help themselves. Everyone needs to realise this – and it is a very sobering thought.

Worsening inequality

The debt crisis also highlights another related problem, viz. that there is a growing amount of inequality within our own society. More and more people seem to be living at the limit, or beyond the limit, of their own earning capacity – so that a sudden change in circumstances can leave them almost destitute. The uncomfortable statistic is that about 20% of people in the UK are currently living in poverty.[17]

This trend can be seen for example in the increasing number of people making use of foodbanks in the UK. It may be quite a surprise for many people to learn that the Trussell Trust foodbank network, a Christian charity, gave emergency food to 128,697 people in the UK in 2011-12, and 346,992 in 2012-13. As well as providing emergency food, the Trussell Trust also gives encouragement to poverty-stricken families and educative support in the form of 'Eat well, spend less' courses.[18]

Other charities also exist to help people find their way out of "the black hole of debt". The charity, Christians Against Poverty (CAP), serves people by helping them work out fair budgets,

---

[17] according to World Health Organisation criteria
[18] http://www.trusselltrust.org/

negotiate with creditors, as well as take them through insolvency procedures. CAP also run courses, in partnership with local churches, and are teaching 10,000 people a year how to budget, save and prevent debt. In addition, they have launched job clubs.[19]

Easy money

The moneylenders, including the banks, seem only too prepared these days to let people borrow money, and this is facilitated by interest rates being so low. The pressures on people to take out credit will be discussed in a later chapter, but first of all it is illuminating to look at a graph of the amount of money in circulation in the economy - as given by the so-called M4 money supply - compared to the total amount of personal debt in the country.[20] The diagram on the next page reveals some very important relationships. Firstly, notice that the amount of money in the economy increased at a huge rate throughout the two decades from 1990 to 2010, and it took an even greater upwards turn in about 2005. Clearly, anyone seeing a graph of this nature will realise that this growth in the money supply is unsustainable. Something is going to have to give, and it did give! We had the economic crisis and recession.

The next question to ask is, where did all this extra money come from? The answer is that the banks created it.....out of nothing. They (simply) created money electronically to lend to borrowers, without having the necessary liquidity to back it up. This is an incredible "ruse" that will be discussed in more detail in Chapter 13. As we see from the graph, the amount of personal debt rose in tandem with the excessive increase in the money supply. This is the legacy of the "debt money system" caused by fractional reserve lending that I will describe later.

---

[19] https://capuk.org/
[20] M4 is derived from the consolidated balance sheet of UK monetary financial institutions

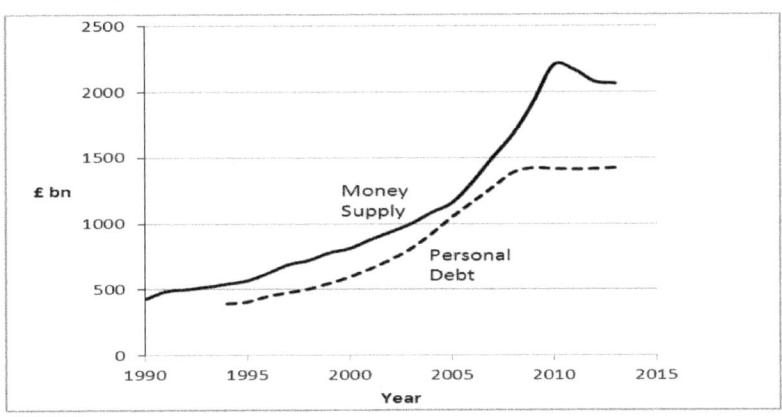

Fig.9.1 Money Supply M4 and UK Personal Debt (1993-2013)

The relatively small difference between personal debt and money supply seems to be around £200 billion. This is (simplistically) the amount of money issued by the Bank of England that is in circulation as notes and coins. From the graph we can also see the effect on the money supply caused by QE, which increased M4 in the year 2009 by an extra 200 to 300 billion pounds. The vast majority of the money supply, however, 97% of it currently, is debt money created and issued by private banks as loans.

Conclusion

We can summarise by saying that under "normal" or "healthy" economic circumstances there is around two-hundred billion pounds in circulation in the economy. The sharp increase in the money supply recently is due almost entirely to the irresponsible increase in high-street bank lending in the late nineties and early part of this century. In 2009 the money supply leapt by a further few hundred billion pounds, which is the result of the Bank of England's quantitative easing programme. The correlation between personal debt and money supply is very strong, as can be seen by the graph. Fortunately, the uncontrolled upward trend now seems to have been stopped.

WAR ON DEBT

Chapter 10: ON THE INEQUALITY OF INCOME

"It must be apparent to every thinking person that something is very wrong in the United States. Chaos, crime and revolutionary activity are mounting everywhere. Inflation continues to erode the value of the dollar and our constitutional rights are being systematically stripped from us. In the midst of a nation which is capable of creating abundance, we are faced with a situation where over ninety per cent of the wealth of the nation is controlled by less than one per cent of its citizens." - June Grem

Preamble

The above is a short extract from the Preface of a classic book, *The Money Manipulators,* written by June Grem in 1971. So, what's new, you might ask? Not a lot, in some respects. In fact, in the meantime wealth inequality has become even worse in most of the western world (not just in the USA), and it has become even more urgent to tackle this important issue of unfairness in society. Indeed, one of the main factors involved in the social unrest we saw in the UK in August 2011 can probably be summed up in that single word, inequality. Many people on low incomes or no income at all have the perception that society is unfair, and I would agree with them. Society is definitely unfair, and it always will be, to some extent. However, in recent years it has become increasingly and excessively unfair, despite the fact that we have a democratic government and do not live in a dictatorship or feudal society. In other words, no free society is going to have a situation where all members of it earn an equal standard of living, but the inequality in the UK is too great now, and has been getting worse year by year. This wealth inequality has driven people into increasing their personal debt as they strive by any means possible to improve their superficial standard of living.

Wealth and income

Wealth and income are obviously not synonymous, so it is best to differentiate between these two terms straight away. While the two concepts go hand-in-hand it is often misleading to use them interchangeably. Income could be defined as the amount of money one receives on a regular basis, whereas wealth is essentially the amount of money and possessions one has accumulated. On this basis, although most pensioners have a relatively small income compared to most working people, they may in fact be relatively wealthy. For example, the combined income - in the form of pensions - of my wife and myself is approximately one-fifth or only 20% of the current combined incomes of my son and daughter-in-law. Yet, we do not feel poverty-stricken compared to them, because we own the house we live in and have much lower outgoings than they do. Potentially, though, they are much wealthier than we are, especially if future inflation erodes the spending power of our pensions and savings when we get too old to be able to do anything about it.

In this chapter, however, I only want to discuss the issue of income inequality, because in the long term it is primarily the income that one receives throughout one's working life that finally determines one's wealth. There are in addition of course an enormous number of other factors that play a significant rôle, including the government's taxation policy and one's individual spending habits.

Overcoming income inequality

Fortunately we have a statistical indicator that measures income inequality in an entirely objective way. This is the *Gini coefficient*, which is a quantity that characterises the complete income distribution of the households of a country (or any group) by means of a single number that can range from 0 to 1: the higher the number, the greater the degree of income inequality. Zero corresponds to the situation where every household would have an equal income (per individual), whereas a value of 1 corresponds to inequality in its most extreme form, with a single individual having all the income in the economy.[21]

The next figure shows the evolution of the Gini coefficient for households in Great Britain since 1979. We see from this very clearly how income inequality rose considerably over the period when Margaret Thatcher was Prime Minister in the 1980s, from around 0.25 in 1979 to a peak of around 0.34 in the early 1990s. The Institute for Fiscal Studies points out that this is an unparalleled rise in inequality, both historically and compared to the changes in other developed nations, although the United States has also experienced a similarly sharp increase in inequality.

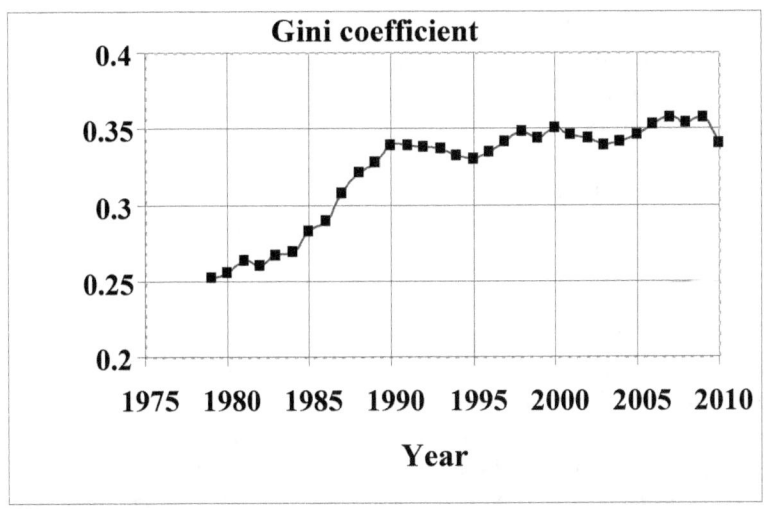

Fig. 10.1: The Gini Coefficient for disposable income for households in Great Britain from 1979 to 2010 (Source of data: Institute for Fiscal Studies)

Since the early 1990s, the changes in income inequality have been less marked. After falling slightly over the early to mid-1990s, inequality rose again during New Labour's first term of office, with

---

[21] The basis for calculating the Gini coefficient can be found on the Wikipedia website http://en.wikipedia.org/wiki/Gini_coefficient

the Gini coefficient reaching a new peak of 0.35 in 2000-01. During Labour's second term of office, the Gini coefficient fell slightly, with the level of inequality in 2003-04 returning to that last seen in 1997-98, so that over the first two terms of the Labour government the net effect of these changes was to leave income inequality largely unchanged, but at historically high levels. Income inequality then rose in each of the first three years of Labour's third term in government. This left the Gini coefficient at 0.36, its highest level since time-series data were first obtained in 1961. Recently, however, the IFS have reported that the Gini coefficient decreased strongly from 0.36 to 0.34 in the first year since the Coalition came to power (2010-11 data point), and more recently it has been reported to be approximately as low as 0.32.

Driving this recent drop in income inequality has been the fact that recession-related falls in real incomes have been smallest towards the bottom of the income distribution and largest towards the top.[22] In other words, the wealthy suffered larger drops in income on average than the poor - which could be regarded as a good thing. The question is, when the economy does recover, will the rich regain their excessive incomes at the expense of the poor, or not?

The Gini coefficient as an index of inequality can provide an objective measure that could help the Chancellor of the Exchequer adjust the burden of taxation in such a way that disposable income or take-home pay appears fair to a maximum number of people. The Chancellor should therefore use his budget powers over the levels of income tax to reduce this inequality of disposable income back to the values it had before Thatcherism, and preferably to Gini levels even more equitable than that. Using the raw data on the present income distribution, it would not be difficult to calculate a progression formula (sliding-scale) for income tax levels whose outcome would result in a Gini coefficient of 0.25, for instance. This would then compare favourably with the period in Britain before Thatcherism, and be similar to the level today in some developed western European

---

[22] IFS Commentary C124: "Living standards, poverty and inequality in the UK:2012" Jonathan Cribb, Robert Joyce, David Philip (June 2012)

countries such as Denmark and Norway, as well as Japan. Even a drop to 0.30 would be a considerable improvement, which is approximately the value presently shown by countries such as Italy, Sweden and Germany.

In order to achieve a lower Gini coefficient for disposable income than at present, it is clear that higher earners would need to be taxed more, while low earners would be taxed less, and some even have their pay supplemented. One of the Lib Dems' aims under Nick Clegg was to absolve anyone with an income of less than £10,000 per annum from paying income tax at all. However, this aim is not specifically a current policy of the Conservative-led Coalition.

Readjusting the income tax burden does not mean *per se* that taxation has to be increased overall. The income tax burden could just be re-weighted in favour of a more equal society. High earners will "puff and blow" about this, but they need to realise that the social benefits will ultimately far outweigh their personal greed. One of the underlying reasons the country has been hit by riots, and that we have a "broken society", as Mr Cameron calls it, is due to the overwhelming feeling of inequality and unfairness that has gradually been coming to the surface in the country ever since the days of Margaret Thatcher as Prime Minister.

Apart from the government attempting to reduce the inequality in disposable income via progressive taxation, the feeling of fairness needs to extend right down to the pay structure of all organisations. A celebrity footballer, pocketing in one week what most people can only earn in a year, is an example of how incomes have become distorted in the UK. If top footballers were paid less, the tickets to watch matches would be cheaper, and our clubs would not have to be bought up by foreign business moguls. Of course the above example itself is not very representative, since footballers must make the most of their small window of opportunity to earn large sums of money when they are young and fit enough to entertain the public. But what about TV celebrities, senior lawyers, hospital consultants, top bankers and company directors, etc.? Their incomes are often disproportionately exaggerated. Even within the public service there is a huge difference in pay between top civil servants and those doing more menial tasks. The income inequality in these organisations also needs to be tackled via the same principle as above. I think it would be a good idea if the government required every company or organisation to publish its own distribution of salaries and to calculate its corresponding Gini coefficient. If it exceeded the benchmark figure of 0.25, the company or organisation should be obliged to correct its pay structure accordingly.

Even for the employees of a small business, there should be a regime of fair incomes. Take, for example, just three people being paid £10k, £30k and £60k per year. The Gini coefficient is mathematically equivalent to half the relative mean difference between the values. The absolute mean difference in this example is £33.3k, and the relative mean difference is this divided by the mean salary which is also £33.3k. So the Gini coefficient for this distribution is exactly 0.50, which is much higher than the benchmark figure of 0.25. To reduce this distribution to a Gini coefficient of 0.25, keeping the total amount paid the same and the middle income the same, we would need to adjust the salaries to be £22.5k, £30k and £47.5k. (You can easily check this for yourself!) The lowest paid would see their income more than double in this example, the median stays the same, and the highest paid would have a considerably reduced salary. That is the best way to create an equitable society. There is still the incentive to be ambitious and get paid more, but the lower paid would not have a feeling of unfairness or that they are being exploited.

Interestingly, in an initiative by Switzerland's Young Socialists a referendum was held at the end of November 2013 to try to curb the pay differential between top managers and the lowest paid workers. The chief executive of Novartis, for example, is paid 15.7 million Swiss francs annually, whereas the lowest salary in the firm is 59 thousand francs, which is a ratio of 266:1. The measures, if they had been approved, would have limited salaries of top managers to no more than 12 times the wage of the low-paid workers in the same company. Unfortunately, the reform was turned down by the Swiss electorate. It would have signalled a major step towards greater income equality, had it been accepted.

Conclusion

Since it is notoriously difficult for governments to implement the income tax changes that would be needed to create an equitable society, a pathway to a fairer society could be achieved via governmental control of the distribution of income. Legislation could be passed requiring every company and organisation to adopt a wages policy that delivered a Gini coefficient of 0.25 or lower. This has no effect on the total wage bill of a company or organisation; it simply provides for a fairer balance of salaries or wages. This measure would undoubtedly have a very positive social impact.

Chapter 11: PRICE INFLATION

"Oh, people can come up with statistics to prove anything, Kent. 14% of people know that." - *Homer Simpson*

Preamble

The government attempts to steer economic output and employment via the Bank of England's monetary policy on interest rates. Traditionally, high interest rates bring about a dampening of inflation. At the moment, however, we have an ostensibly *anomalous* situation in that very low interest rates are being accompanied by quite a low inflation rate. This has been explained by saying that cuts and high unemployment are deflationary, but the inflation rate will take off when there is more employment, and consumer confidence improves. At that point the BoE will start to raise interest rates to ward off the galloping inflation that is just waiting in the sidelines.

Inflation target

An explicit inflation target was first set in October 1992 by the then Chancellor of the Exchequer, Norman Lamont, following the UK's departure from the European Exchange Rate Mechanism (ERM). The target was based on the RPIX, which is the RPI calculated excluding mortgage interest payments.[23]

Until 1997, Sterling interest rates were set by the Treasury. On election in May 1997, the Labour government of Tony Blair with Gordon Brown as Chancellor of the Exchequer handed control over interest rates to the Bank of England Monetary Committee, which was given the responsibility of adjusting interest

---

[23] This was felt to be a better measure of the effectiveness of macroeconomic policy; it was argued that if interest rates are used to curb inflation, then including mortgage payments in the inflation measure would be misleading.

rates in order to meet an inflation target set by the Chancellor. The initial target rate of inflation was an RPIX of 2.5%. The committee always meets once per month to decide if any changes to the interest rate are necessary. If, in any month, inflation deviates from the target by more than one percent, the Governor of the Bank of England (BoE) is required to write an open letter to the Chancellor explaining the reasons for this and to propose a plan of action for bringing inflation back towards the target. This will be discussed in more detail later.

Since 1996, the United Kingdom government has also calculated the CPI, and in December 2003, the inflation target was changed officially to a CPI of 2%, from the previous RPIX target of 2.5%. The CPI, RPIX, and RPI are published monthly by the Office for National Statistics (ONS). There is usually, but not always, a small difference between the different indices.

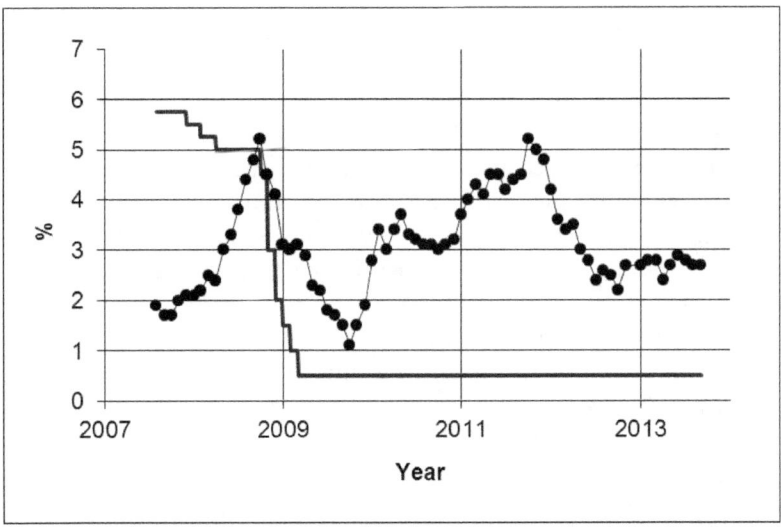

Fig. 11.1: *CPI (dots, annual increase) and the Bank of England base rate (continuous line) in % from 2007-2013*

The above diagram shows the CPI and BoE base rate from the middle of 2007 up to the present (September 2013). As the economic downturn due to the financial crisis unfolded towards the end of 2007, the BoE lowered the base rate rapidly from almost 6% to just 0.5%, where it has stayed ever since. The CPI on the other hand has oscillated between about 1 and 5%. At present the CPI is in line with the government's inflation target of 2% with a leeway of ±1%.

<u>What is really happening?</u>

My explanation of the "anomalous situation" in the above Preamble is based on what you could call conventional wisdom. However, I think it falls very short of being a proper explanation, because the inflation statistic CPI does not expose a very strong underlying phenomenon that has either been suppressed or not understood, to date!

The latest official figures for October 2013 claim that UK annual inflation is running at a CPI of 2.2%. Previously it had allegedly been about 2.7% for quite some time. However, every ordinary shopper and householder in the country knows that prices are rising on average by far more than that small percentage: in the five years from 2007-2012, for example, the CPI increased by 17%, whereas gas prices rose 46%, vehicle tax and insurance 88%, fuel by 56% and food by 30%. At the same time wages rose by only 10% on average. Over the ten years from 2002-2012, the CPI rose by 29%, whereas gas prices increased by 142%, vehicle tax and insurance by 108%, fuel by 71% and food by 43%; wages increased by 36% over that period. In other words, the cost of living is far outstripping the CPI.

Indeed, most people are painfully aware that the cost of ordinary essential commodities, such as fuel, food, council tax and housing, have all been increasing on average over many years far more than the official inflation figures claim. Hence it is understandable if we, the ordinary consumers, are sceptical about the government's inflation figures.

I therefore decided to look into this phenomenon, to try to understand what is really going on, and to assess the implications of this discrepancy between official economic figures and the perceptions of the general public. It soon became clear that we have what could be called a bifurcation between the prices of essential items (such as food, fuel and housing) and non-essential items (such as large cars, the latest electronic gadgets, holidays abroad, and other luxuries). This is a phenomenon that has been given the name biflation.

Biflation

Biflation (sometimes called mixflation) is a state of the economy where processes of inflation and deflation occur simultaneously. The term seems to have been first introduced in America by F.Osborne Brown in the year 2003.[24] During biflation there is an inflationary rise in the price of commodity-based assets (i.e., essentials) and a simultaneous fall in the price of debt-based assets (non-essentials).

The prices for all assets are based on the demand for them versus the volume of money in circulation to buy them. Biflation occurs because of the following two competing factors: when the economy is being fuelled by an over-abundance of money injected into the economy by the banks (as now), essential commodities remain in high demand, and so the prices rise simply due to the increased volume of money chasing them.[25] The increasing costs to purchase these essentials forms the inflationary arm of biflation. On the other hand, the economy is being held back by unemployment and decreasing disposable income, so that a greater proportion of money is directed at purchasing essential items and away from non-essentials. Debt-based assets (luxuries) thus fall into lower demand, and drop in price (or do not increase so markedly). The decreasing costs to purchase these non-essentials is the deflationary arm of biflation. This is clearly a highly simplified

---

[24] http://en.wikipedia.org/wiki/Biflation
[25] This is one of the reasons house prices have been so over-inflated: because very large mortgages have been easy to come by.

explanation, but suitable enough to understand the basic principles.

The question whether an item is essential or non-essential – which is very important for the consumer – is simply not encapsulated within the CPI. Essential prices may be rising alarmingly while non-essentials drop in price. The CPI merely gives some sort of bland average of these two factors. The basic problem is that we have in reality a strongly biflationary economy. At present the CPI (and RPI) seems to lie at about one half of the value for the inflationary index of essentials.

Stefanie Flanders, the former BBC correspondent, suggested recently that the ONS might regard it as being better to be "consistent rather than right", when it comes to the price indices. Should we simply accept that these are just statistical quantities? No, we shouldn't. It is crucial to get it right, because state pensions and salaries are index-linked, previously to the RPI, and now to the CPI. This means that, since the indices consistently understate inflation in essential commodities, a large proportion of often the least well-off people have an income that is gradually lagging behind real price rises, or a purchasing power that is decreasing. This is worsening the wealth inequality in the country.

Conclusion

For reasons of equity, the government should require that price indices truly reflect the rise in average prices of *essentia* goods and services. The lag of index-linked pensions and salaries, especially in the state sector, has caused much industrial unrest and antipathy in the past, and is the reason why trade unions and government could hardly ever agree amicably on wage increases. In effect, pensioners, savers and workers are being "conned" by the official inflation figures, against which they have as yet failed to formulate a coherent argument.

Chapter 12: MONETARY REFORM

"Hey, man, this is a great ruse. Printing money is a lot easier than doing productive work." - Anonymous

Preamble

Six years after the start of the current financial crisis, politicians, economists, the general public and the media seem to be waking up to the urgent need to reform the banking system. This chapter is about the money supply and how the behaviour of the banks crucially affects the economy and ultimately the well-being of all of us. We shall see that the ingenious trick by the banks of lending money they haven't got creates wealth for bankers and misery for the rest of us.

In this chapter, I shall introduce our strategy for fighting debt by briefly raising the issue at two levels. Firstly we must understand the way our monetary system works in order to understand how debt originates, before we can even hope to begin eradicating it. Secondly, we need to change our attitude to production, so that we can act properly to maintain the basic wealth and prosperity of our society.

Food for thought

In the past couple of years several organisations, including *Positive Money*, have been helpful in illuminating the issue of how money is actually created. It turns out that their insight is by no means new. For example, as long ago as 1934 the American, Robert Hemphill, wrote the following (quoted in Irving Fisher's book entitled *100% Money*): "*Someone has to borrow every dollar we have in circulation. If the banks create ample money, we are prosperous. If not, we starve. When one gets a complete grasp of the picture, the tragic absurdity of our hopeless position is incredible. It is the most important subject intelligent persons can investigate and reflect upon.*"

The meaning of the above paragraph may not be clear until I explain what occurs. When a government borrows money it does so by selling interest-bearing bonds, which are called government bonds or gilts in the UK. Let us stay with America for the time being. In the video documentary *The impending collapse of the world economy*[26] the commentator illustrates what happens via the following example: "*When a US bank buys a $100 bond, it gets to loan out 10 times that amount, so the bank not only gets back the $100 plus interest of $6 from the Federal Government, it gets to loan out another $1,000 it doesn't have, and charge $60 additional interest. Banks are allowed to create this extra money out of thin air. That's why bank buildings are way the biggest in every town on the planet. This system of lending more than you have is called fractional reserve lending.*"

I must admit it took me quite some time after first hearing about this concept for its main implications to dawn on me. What you have in effect is banks lending us money electronically that they do not actually possess. This is clearly contrary to what we might naively imagine, viz. that banks only lend money that has been deposited by someone else (called full-reserve lending). The more money that banks lend, the more income they obtain from the interest we pay them, so, as a result of the lack of liquidity requirements imposed upon them, banks are tempted to lend more than they should. Coupled with this, the very low interest rates in operation tempt us to borrow from the banks a lot more than we should as well.

---

[26] http://www.youtube.com/watch?v=YdYG_ZEw2xw

WAR ON DEBT

This is essentially the root cause of much of our debt and our consequent financial woes today. In particular, the financial crisis that unfolded first in the USA in 2007-2008 was caused substantially by banks making loans to people who had difficulty keeping up with their repayments, and who defaulted on their loans. These so-called subprime loans are characterized by relatively high interest rates, poor collateral and less favorable terms in order to compensate for high credit risk. Many subprime loans were packaged into mortgage-backed securities (MBS).[27]

London's Canary Wharf business district, viewed from Greenwich (photograph taken by David Owen)

Continuing with this incredible realisation about what banks actually do, I happened to stumble upon the following article, which frankly took my breath away. Here is a short extract from the first chapter: "*We, all of British blood and descent, having studied the causes of the present world unrest have long been forced to the conclusion that an essential first step towards*

---
[27] A security or financial instrument is a tradable asset of any kind

the return of human happiness and brotherhood with economic security and liberty of life and conscience, such as will permit the Christian ethic to flourish again, is the immediate resumption by the community in each nation of its prerogative over the issue of money, including its modern credit substitutes. This prerogative has been usurped by those still termed in general 'bankers', both national and international, who have perfected a technique to enable themselves to create the money they lend by the granting of bookkeeping credits, and to destroy it by the withdrawal of the latter at their discretion, in accordance with entirely mistaken and obsolete ideas which they do not defend against impartial and informed scientific criticism and examination. In this way a form of national money debt has been invented, in which the lender surrenders nothing at all; and which it is physically an impossibility for the community ever to pay."

The above paragraph is a quote from a letter to church dignitaries jointly written by a number of leading experts. It was written as long ago as 1943, during the Second World War. The book in which the quote is to be found is entitled *Money Manipulation and Social Order*, and was written by The Rev Denis Fahey, an Irish priest. Its message seems strangely familiar and relevant today.

The money supply

Monetary policy in the UK is the process whereby the Bank of England controls the supply of money in the economy, and its cost, via the rate of interest. An expansionary policy (involving increasing the money supply) is traditionally used to combat unemployment in a recession by reducing interest rates. This is the situation today, where the Bank of England has reduced its base rate at present to the historically low level of 0.5%. On the other hand, a contractionary policy (decrease of the money supply) involves raising interest rates in order to combat inflation.

This thinking is based on the correlation between money supply and inflation. It is not necessarily a very good correlation, as I have shown in a previous chapter, but you could imagine, for example, that if you suddenly doubled the amount of money in circulation, within a very short time prices would have doubled too, and your pound would only buy half as much quantity of goods. Governments who print money, thus devalue the currency.[28]

These days, as we have already discovered, governments do not physically have to print notes and mint coins in order for the money in circulation to increase. This is done by the private banks, and is essentially the same as the fractional reserve lending I described earlier. Most people might think that when they deposit £100 in their current account, for instance, the bank somehow keeps this money locked up in a vault for them to withdraw at any time. However, in practice, there is the so-called reserve requirement or liquidity ratio to consider. In the UK the liquidity ratio was 20.5% in 1968. This means that the bank was obliged to keep 20.5% of your money in reserve, whereas it could temporarily invest the remainder. As financial institutions have been deregulated over the past few decades, the cash reserve requirement of banks has also dropped markedly: 20.5% in 1968, 15.9% in 1978, 5% in 1988, and since 1998 it has stood at only 3.1%. This is apparently a voluntary figure, and there is no compulsion about it. This very small level of liquidity ratio means that banks can now have a bonanza by being able to generate up to 32 times as much money as was originally deposited. The downside would be if everyone wanted their money back in a hurry. If this occurred, the banks would not have enough liquidity – which is essentially what happened during the credit squeeze of 2007. The virtual money created by the banks had, of course, already been cashed as real money by the recipients, which meant that the banks had a huge latent debt. In other words, they became insolvent, leading amongst other things to the necessity for government bailouts. The alternative would have been for the government to let the banks default on their debts. (The above

---

[28] This is the tragic situation that recently occurred in Zimbabwe. Someone I met a couple of years ago showed me a one billion Zimbabwean Dollar note, which he said would just about buy him a loaf of bread (in the morning). The most well known example of hyper-inflation – leading to the rise of Hitler – was of course that occurring in Germany between the two world wars.

discussion is admittedly simplistic, but it was just used to make a few simple points.)

Quantitative easing

I wrote the last section without even mentioning the very important way in which the Bank of England has recently been manipulating the money supply. Faced with virtually no more leeway to lower interest rates in order to stimulate the economy (the current base-rate value of 0.5% is essentially as low as it can go)[29], it has been "pumping new money into the economy" by buying assets such as government bonds and bonds issued by big companies, as a way of boosting lending by commercial banks. It does this essentially by crediting its own bank account. In this way it has already created £375 billion (or roughly £15,000 per household). The shrewd thing about this form of money manipulation is that it doesn't directly increase the national debt.

In theory the commercial banks then lend this extra money to companies and individuals, who in turn spend the money on things like expanding businesses, buying new homes, etc., which should boost the economy. Then, again theoretically, when the recession is over and the economy has recovered, the Bank of England sells the bonds back to the banks and "destroys" the cash it receives, which means that in the long term no extra money has been created.

The danger is that QE will ultimately cause the rate of inflation to rise steeply, rather like it would by simply printing money. When, or whether, the Bank of England will destroy the extra cash again is an unanswerable question at present.

Reforming the banks

It could be argued that the UK's five major banks taken together are more powerful than the government and the Bank of England, since they control 85% of the financial markets and are

---

[29] The European Central Bank has just lowered its lending rate to 0.25%, and some countries' central banks even have a base rate of 0%!

responsible for creating 97% of the money supply. It has now become clear that the financial crisis of 2007-2008 occurred because we (the public, including the government) failed to constrain the creation of money for lending. Even with this knowledge, Britain's public debt still continues to increase. It is blatantly obvious that the country desperately needs politicians, civil servants, financial advisors and economic experts who thoroughly understand the economics of the monetary system, and who are willing to act to prevent the situation spiralling even further out of control. Furthermore the general public are woefully unaware of the consequences of banks being able to create money, a power that is turning out to be the root cause of many of the economic and social miseries facing millions of people in this country today, as well as globally.

The research and campaign organisation *Positive Money*[30] has done much to illuminate the issue of money creation and how this led to the financial crisis of 2007-2008. First of all, it may surprise the reader to learn that only 3% of the money in the economy is actually issued by the Bank of England (BoE) in the form of coins and notes; 97% of the money in circulation is electronic money created by the high-street banks. When one takes out a loan from a bank, it just creates the money. Of course, if an individual were to do this, he or she would be arrested and put in prison. However, banks can do this with impunity.

I think most people still have an old-fashioned concept of banking. We go cap in hand to our local bank manager and beg for a loan to buy a house or a car. If our financial situation is such that the friendly bank manager - who has personally known our family for at least the past twenty years - thinks we shall be capable of paying back the loan within the allotted time, then he will sanction the request. We go away imagining that the money we are borrowing has somehow been deposited by someone else in a savings or deposit account, or that the bank has in any case enough gold or silver in its vaults to cover the loan should we not be able to pay it back. The truth is very far from that at present: banks have

---

[30] www.positivemoney.org.uk

virtually no liquidity or reserve funds to cover loans. The money is essentially created when a loan is taken out.

The obvious downside of this creation of money is that it leads to inflation, or a devaluation of the pound in your pocket. The BoE tries to control inflation by adjusting interest rates, and it should be said that, although the money supply has increased a great deal recently, inflation has been much lower. The orthodox reason for this is that the economy is depressed, i.e., we are in or near a state of recession, which means lack of demand is the reason for prices not increasing more rapidly than you would expect from the increase in the money supply. However, ordinary consumer prices have risen much more than the official index states, as I have shown, There is now a strong danger too - already built in by the policy of allowing the money supply to increase - that when the economy does come out of recession, inflation will increase dramatically.

Under the present, outdated economic system, lending money is regarded as a means of expanding the economy, but the salutory fact at present (according to *Positive Money*) is that only 8% of money borrowed is actually invested in productive activities that help the country's GDP to increase, while 92% goes towards non-GDP business, such as house price bubbles and financial speculation. The £375 billion of quantitative easing carried out by the BoE is in my opinion so unfocused that it does not really have the effect that is required, i.e., it is a very expensive and inefficient way of trying to stimulate the economy. Imagine what you could do with all that created money if you earmarked it for specific projects that boosted jobs and industry directly!

Housing and mortgages

The private borrowing in the country can be broken down into four sectors: 10% for consumer finance; 40% housing; 13% non-financial, and 37% in the financial sector. The largest sector for borrowing is the housing market. The reason that there has been a threefold increase in house prices over the past twenty years - well above wage inflation - is not due to the conventional view that there is a housing shortage, but mainly due to the fact that there has been so much mortgage lending. House prices are at present about double what they should be compared to earnings, and it is clear that many (especially young) people are finding it difficult to step onto the housing ladder. What was happening before the credit crunch was that vast mortgages were too easy to come by, inevitably pushing up house prices.

Since borrowing has become more difficult recently, there are moves to help first-time buyers continue to obtain massive mortgages. For example, a scheme has recently been started called *Help to Buy*. There are currently two variants of the scheme available, both requiring just a 5% deposit and offered to first-time buyers as well as existing homeowners. A 'Help to Buy Equity Loan' is available on newly built homes up to £600,000 in England and £400,000 in Scotland. The borrower only needs to secure up to a 75% mortgage from a bank or building society. The Government will then lend an equity loan of up to 20% of the property value, which can be repaid at any time or on the sale of the house. In England, this equity loan is interest free for the first five years. Alternatively, the 'Help to Buy Mortgage Guarantee' is available on new homes and existing homes up to £600,000 in England, Scotland and Wales. A 95% mortgage from a participating lender is required, where the lender can offer this higher loan-to-value mortgage, as the government will provide the lender with a guarantee of up to 15% of the property value.

Ironically, I feel this is exactly the wrong approach to take. It actually exacerbates the problem overall and in the longer term. Governments seem unable to learn! Making large mortgages much more accessible to people has the effect of inflating house prices, so that houses become even more unaffordable. The clever approach would be to do exactly the opposite, viz. legislate to make 90-100% mortgages extremely difficult or even impossible to obtain. This would then tend to slow down the housing market, and ultimately lead to lower prices. Then, and only then, would first-time buyers stand a chance of being able to buy a house which they can truly afford - with a much lower level of debt. In fact, the common perception - that it is a good thing for house prices to be rising - is extremely misguided as far as the ordinary person is concerned. It really only benefits the money manipulators, and is essentially what caused the subprime mortgage crisis just a few years ago!

Coupled to this, however, there is a drastic need in this country for more rented accommodation, so that young people in particular do not have to commit themselves to buying a property so early on in their lives. A change in attitude is necessary, in that rented housing should not be looked upon as inferior or infra dig. A great folly occurred when Mrs Thatcher sold off Britain's council housing stock with a view to gaining cheap revenue for the Treasury, without making adequate provision for the demand in rented accommodation that would inevitably follow. Not everyone actually wants to own their own home, especially when they are in a career situation that might require job mobility. In this respect Britain should look to the continent of Europe, where in most countries it is quite normal for people to rent.

Summary: the rules of the game

From the above discussion we may summarise the elementary rules of our current monetary system, as follows: the greater the amount of money there is in circulation, the greater is the level of debt; but the corollary of this ridiculous situation is that less debt means we have less money, so we are poorer. What we really need is more money combined with less debt, which is impossible under the present system.

The organisation *Positive Money* therefore concludes we must remove the power of the banks to create money out of loans, because banks will inherently create too much money for the wrong things, not for the the best reasons (such as to lend to industries that create jobs). Instead, only the BoE should be able to create money, and bank lending should only come from (a) money that banks can raise from stock markets, (b) customers via investment accounts (deposit accounts, but not current accounts), and (c) loans from the BoE. In essence, the power to create money must be returned to the state. This money must then only be used

to do the right things for the benefit of the country as a whole, namely to:
- spend more on public services
- cut taxes
- reduce the national debt, or
- just be given back to the people (£375 billion of QE could have created jobs for lots of people, in fact, all of the currently unemployed for 5 years).

There is, however, a central problem of "mentality". If the BoE directs lending only to productive activity, we run into the classical problem of central planning or interference from the state. The question then arises: why should a central planner know better than individuals what the proper volume and direction of lending should be? It is not a satisfactory reply to say that the financial crisis has proved that individuals' judgements are flawed; the crisis did not happen because individual borrowers borrowed too much. It happened because of poor decisions by individual banks – being too dependent on wholesale funding in the cases of Northern Rock and Bradford & Bingley; and deciding to take over ABM Amro in the case of RBS. The real problem is that individuals in the banks were, and still are, too greedy. They realise that the interest they can obtain from (almost) unrestricted lending can be invested to make even bigger profits and reap even bigger bonuses. It is not going to be easy to alter the mentality of bankers who are only exploiting the current system to their own maximum advantage. This situation can only be altered by government legislation to change the monetary system.

What is happening now regarding bank reform?

Government measures

A number of government measures have been brought into play since the most recent banking crisis, and the financial sector is now under more scrutiny than ever.[31] Let us remind ourselves that the banking system was saved from collapse by billions of pounds of taxpayers' money, and the public are angry with bankers for taking risks and being too greedy, in particular on the issue of pay and bonuses.

As a result, in December 2010 European regulators announced restrictions on the bonuses that banks can pay their staff. Now they can only receive 20-30% of their bonuses in immediate cash. The guidelines require banks to defer 40-60% of bonuses for three to five years and pay 50% of bonuses in shares, set a maximum bonus level as a percentage of pay, and publish the details for senior management. Regulators have also encouraged banks to "claw back" pay if an individual banker's performance is later deemed not to be worthy of the pay. Lloyds has cut £2 million from bonuses paid to 13 executives regarding the mis-selling of payment protection insurance, for example, and JPMorgan says it will claw back £3.7 billion from individuals responsible for losses caused by trading in complex financial derivatives.

In January 2011 the Chancellor brought in a bank levy (in cooperation with Germany and France) on the largest banks, which is an annual tax on their balance sheets, amounting to 0.04% originally, and which increased to 0.088% in January 2012. This was intended to raise about £8 billion for the Treasury over four years, as well as discourage banks from relying on risky forms of borrowing which were blamed for making the financial crisis more dangerous, and to compensate the taxpayer somewhat for bailing out the banks.

An independent enquiry was set up by the Government to examine the banking system, led by Sir John Vickers. The idea was to ring-fence banks' retail business from their riskier investment operations. Following the Vickers Commission recommendations, the government drafted a bill on banking reform, which the Parliamentary Commission on Banking Standards criticised as falling "well short of what is required". Consequently the government agreed to "electrify" the ring-fence, which means that a bank that fails to separate its retail and investment arms would be

---

[31] http://www.bbc.co.uk/news/business-20811289

broken up. As well as ring-fencing, the bill aims to rank retail deposits but not pension liabilities ahead of the claims of other bank creditors in the event of a bank's insolvency. It will also require banks to hold a sufficient capital buffer so that if they do fail, losses can be absorbed. The bill has now gone before the UK Parliament.

In addition, significant changes to the regulatory system of the UK's financial sector have been announced over the past couple of years. The Financial Services Act will replace the current structure made up of the Financial Services Authority (FSA), The Treasury and the Bank of England (BoE). In the overhaul, the FSA is to be abolished, and three new bodies created, the first two within the BoE to regulate financial services. These are the Financial Policy Committee (FPC), which has overall responsibility for financial regulation in the UK. It oversees and has the power to instruct two new financial watchdogs: the Prudential Regulation Authority (PRA), which will take over responsibility for supervising the safety and soundness of individual financial firms, and the Financial Conduct Authority (FCA), which will protect consumers from sharp practices, and make sure that workers in the financial services sector comply with rules.

Ordinary savers have long been protected from losing their money if their bank becomes insolvent, but since the onset of the crisis the level of protection has more than doubled. In 2007 the maximum payout for depositors was £31,700 per person; now, under the Financial Services Compensation Scheme, it is £85,000.

Green Investment Bank

The Business Secretary, Vince Cable, recently launched a "Green Investment Bank" (November 2012) with headquarters in Edinburgh. The bank, which was a key pledge of the coalition government, will have £3 billion of government money to invest in areas such as renewable energy, carbon capture and storage, and energy efficiency measures. First to benefit from the fund will be a project in the north east of England that will generate energy from waste. Around £8m will go to the construction of an anaerobic digestion plant on Teesside, the first of six planned over the next five years. This will be matched with a further £8m from the private sector, according to the government. The Green Investment Bank (GIB) will also invest £5m to fit manufacturer Kingspan's UK industrial facilities with systems that will reduce its energy consumption by 15%. Mr Cable said the bank would place the green economy at the heart of the UK's economic recovery, and position the country at the forefront of the drive to develop clean energy. He added that the money "will leverage private sector capital to fund projects in priority sectors from offshore wind to waste and non-domestic energy efficiency, helping to deliver our commitment to create jobs and growth right across the UK."

In order to set up the GIB, however, the UK government had to ensure that the plan to lend for low carbon investment projects did not break EU Commission rules on state aid. Permission to use £3bn of government funds has indeed been granted for four years, but may be withdrawn after that, if lending markets open up to low carbon projects, i.e., it is conditional on lending only to projects that cannot find sufficient funding from commercial markets. The commission in Brussels ruled that the GIB concept had safeguards to avoid the "crowding out" of private investment and preserved a level playing field between competitors. It also foresees the funding would be part of a partnership with private lenders or investors.

British Business Bank

In addition to the above green bank, the Business Secretary has announced (September 2012) that the government is to put £1 billion into setting up a bank designed to increase the amount of lending to small and medium-sized companies, who have struggled for credit since the financial crisis. Mr Cable said that he promised to fight short-termism and get behind good firms. The bank will operate via existing lenders, and start within 18 months. It is hoped the money will be matched by private sector investment. Again the issue of whether it might break EU rules on state lending will have to be overcome for it to go ahead. Government support will be in the form of both guarantees and equity, and will go on to the balance sheet of the new institution and not be reclaimed by the Treasury. It is expected to do this by buying up existing loans that banks have made to such companies. While small businesses would get longer term financial security, the government hopes that its move will free up more capital for the sector. Mr Cable added: "To that end, I believe we need an industrial strategy - a positive and ambitious vision, built around long-term investment and innovation, in skills and science. We are so good at so many things in this country - but for too long the mirage of growth based on property speculation and financial gambling has hidden the harder virtues of making things productively. We must get behind successful British-based firms in vehicles, aerospace, life sciences and creative industries and our world-class scientists and universities." He called for a "will to fight the British curse of short-termism - both in the corporate world and government".

Conclusion

In conclusion, we need a radical reform of the banking system. Since banks tend to take on too much lending, we must insist upon higher capital or liquidity requirements. Since banks are socially irresponsible, we must nationalise them and impose democratic control. Since productive firms are starved of finance, we must create more state investment banks.

In addition to that, we need more education and awareness of the problems in the banking system. The media, such as the BBC, need to improve their understanding and portrayal of economics and banking. Monetary power needs to be transferred in part from the City of London to devolved governments in Cardiff, Edinburgh and Belfast. The WG, for example, should contemplate creating a state Welsh bank that operates on the principle of full-reserve banking and, generally, more green banks and credit unions are needed.

Chapter 13: ALTERNATIVE BANKING

"As a simple countryman, he distrusted the use of money and, finding barter cumbersome, preferred to steal" - Miles Kington, *Welcome to Kington, 1989*

Preamble

Are there ways of bypassing or overcoming the current banking system, so that we are not exploited individually and collectively? There certainly are possibilities opening up. This chapter outlines a few of the more recent initiatives.

Background: fiat money

First of all let us look briefly at some of the basic principles regarding money itself. The fundamental problem with the money supply is related to the issue of fractional reserve lending, as explained previously. However, this in turn is related to the concept of what is called *fiat* money, which I shall discuss briefly below.

Fiat money is essentially money without any intrinsic value (apart from the paper it is written on). This is the case today with all legal tender issued by governments. It is state-issued money which is not convertible by law to any physical object, such as gold or silver, nor fixed in value to any other objective standard. In other words, while gold- or silver-backed representative money entails the legal requirement that the issuing bank redeem it in fixed weights of gold or silver, fiat money's value is unrelated to the value of any physical quantity.

Historically, from 1944 to 1971 the Bretton Woods agreement had fixed the value of one US dollar to 1/35th of an ounce of gold, and other currencies were pegged to the dollar at fixed rates. This gold standard collapsed, however, when the US government ended the convertibility of the US dollar for gold in 1971, in what became known as the Nixon Shock. Since then, all reserve currencies have been fiat currencies, including the US dollar, the pound Sterling and the Euro.

The graph below shows how the gold price has changed subsequent to leaving the gold standard. I think the figure speaks for itself: the dollar has been losing value against gold most of the time, in particular in the early eighties, and then much more markedly from 2005 to 2012.

Fig.13.1   *Gold price in US dollars (1974-2013)*

In the past two years the gold price has been falling back and now stands at $1,244 per ounce.[32] The graph clearly demonstrates how investors tend to buy gold in times of financial crisis, hence pushing its price up. The current drop in the gold price suggests, however, that investors perhaps believe the worst of this financial crisis may now be over, at least for the time being.

As we now know in retrospect, Gordon Brown as Chancellor did what appeared to be a bizarre thing between 1999 and 2002 by selling 400 tonnes of Britain's gold reserves at about the lowest price for over twenty years - between $256 and $296 per ounce. Selling our gold at this stupendously wrong time, cost the British taxpayer billions of pounds, but there were reasons for his

---

[32] http://therealasset.co.uk/charts-and-graph/gold-price-charts/

doing this, apparently. According to Thomas Pascoe of *The Telegraph*[33], Brown was faced with a major dilemma, because even at that time there was the distinct possibility that banks would go bankrupt. The Chancellor took the decision to bail out the banks then by dumping Britain's gold, forcing the price down and allowing the banks to buy back gold at a profit, thus meeting their borrowing obligations! No-one seemed to learn from that situation, however, and the banks were allowed to continue with their irresponsible lending.

Crypto-currencies

How nice it would therefore be if we could devise an infallible monetary system using fiat money, but where the currency could not lose its value or purchasing power due to governments, banks and forgers unscrupulously printing more of it!

Today, monetary economics is a hugely important and dynamic field of study in its own right, of course, and a lot of research has gone into devising possible currencies that could be immune to government manipulation, and where the ordinary person is in control, rather than a central bank. The version of digital currency I would like to mention briefly is the *Bitcoin*[34], which is what is called a *crypto-currency*. The Bitcoin (or BTC) is a unit of digital currency that is "mined" (by analogy with gold) using computer software. This is an algorithm, and the difficulty of mining a Bitcoin is increasing with the number found. At present it is thought that the number of Bitcoins mined has reached about 61% of the absolute maximum total, and that this total of about 21 million will be reached in about the year 2033.

Stefan Molyneux in his video on YouTube, *The Truth about Bitcoin*, explains the concept as follows: "*It is non-hierarchical, not centrally controlled, a voluntary participation of likeminded and talented people, to do something of great value to the world.*"

---

[33] http://blogs.telegraph.co.uk/finance/thomaspascoe/100018367/
[34] weusecoins.com; tryBTC.com

WAR ON DEBT

The point of these Bitcoins is that they can be transmitted at virtually no cost from one Bitcoin address to another in any amount desired, thus bypassing the usual banking system or methods such as Paypal. Addresses are identified by a string of 32 random numbers and letters, similar to a bank account number.

Most of us do not have the facility to mine Bitcoins ourselves, but one can join guilds to mine Bitcoins in a "mining pool" that has the computing capability to do this. Bitcoins cost real money in the sense that they cost electricity in your computer.[35] However, since one does not generally mine Bitcoins oneself, they can be bought on an open financial market – and this is where the link to the real world starts to look somewhat suspicious. The Bitcoin value began very modestly as worth just a few cents, but now it has exploded currently to about 850 US dollars![36] The Bitcoin miners have certainly made their profits without anyone getting their hands dirty or being killed or exploited in a gold mine! Six million of the Bitcoins were mined before the idea "went public", and so it is perfectly clear that the "insiders" have made a great deal of money out of it. In fact, the Bitcoins – which are intrinsically worthless – are selling for real dollars, which could be regarded as a very ingenious form of Ponzi scheme. I therefore feel it is highly unlikely that this concept will ever be used worldwide as a unit of currency, firstly because it seems too intangible and modern for most people to be able to grasp, secondly the value fluctuates wildly, and thirdly I cannot imagine this would not also be subject to fraud, judging by the skilful and inventive criminality of computer hackers.

<u>Lending and borrowing via the Internet</u>

What practical alternatives do we as individuals have for circumventing the current banking system? The internet is coming up with several new platforms enabling individuals to invest and

---

[35] Bitcoinmining.com
[36] the value has suddenly taken off, apparently due to reports that the US government is discussing the idea

borrow money, which could eventually lead to an alternative banking system.

Peer-to-peer lending

Peer-to-peer lending sites, such as *Zopa* and *Funding Circle* have been running successfully for several years. They work by matching online lenders with borrowers, and the interest rates are agreed by the two parties.[37] The lending site *Zopa*, for example, has lent more than £247 million through its website, which states: "At *Zopa*, people who have spare money lend it directly to people who want to borrow. There are no banks in the middle, no huge overheads and no sneaky fees, meaning everyone gets better rates. Voted Moneywise's 'Most Trusted Personal Lender' three years running, *Zopa* is licensed by the Office of Fair Trading and backed by the same investors that backed eBay, Betfair and Skype."[38]

Clearly, there are risks involved when lending money to a site such as *Zopa*, but they take great care to point out that the money you lend is protected in many of the same ways that ordinary banks protect our money. For example, credit checks are made on borrowers, and only those individuals with a good credit rating are allowed to borrow from them. Predictions of "bad debt" are also made, and a factor in favour of lending to sites such as *Zopa* at present is that bad debt has been decreasing markedly over the past few years, from about 5% five years ago to only approximately ½% currently. Money lent to *Zopa* is divided into units of £10 and spread over a large number of borrowers to minimise the effect on the lender of a borrower defaulting. The peer-to-peer system pays for itself by charging the borrower a borrowing fee dependent on the amount borrowed and an annual 1% lender's fee. The overall effect is that the lender receives a higher rate of interest than would be obtained from a high-street bank – mainly because the participants are not paying for bank buildings, staff salaries and large bonuses.

---

[37] Positive News, Issue 73, Autumn 2012, article by Lee Williams
[38] http://uk.zopa.com

WAR ON DEBT

Even the government has now taken an interest in peer-to-peer lending. The Business Secretary, Mr Cable, has announced that the government plans to invest £10 million in *Zopa* in a scheme that is intended to benefit thousands of sole traders, such as builders and other small businesses that are not limited companies, who will now be able to get loans more easily. Another £20 million of taxpayers' money is to be allocated to *Funding Circle* that specialises in limited companies. Disconcerting in my opinion is that Jacob Rothschild, from the famous banking dynasty, has revealed in the last few days that he has bought a stake in *Zopa*, saying "alternative forms of credit will be developed on a significant scale".

Crowdfunding

The story does not end there, however. Other alternative finance models are appearing on the internet. For example, *Seedrs* is a so-called "equity crowdfunding platform" that makes it possible for people to invest even small amounts of money (as little as £10) in business startups. In this way, investing is opening up to a much wider audience and business startups can raise money easily. In other words, the company gives seed-stage entrepreneurs access to a wide pool of equity capital from their friends, family and "the crowds", which is traditionally difficult to come by, and it provides a simple-to-use platform that gives ordinary people access to the financial, personal and professional rewards that come from investing small amounts of money in business startups.

Companies like *Seedrs* are clearly doing this for their own financial benefit: they take a 7.5% fee from entrepreneurs who successfully reach their investment target. Then, if investors are paid dividends, they take a 7.5% fee of all proceeds above and beyond their initial investment. A co-founder of *Seedrs*, Jeff Lynn, in an interview to *Wired.co.uk* stated that, "*As a lawyer I was working with some very large companies and saw just how grossly inefficient and un-innovative they were. I came to understand that value creation in the 21st century is about agility rather than scale,*

111

and that the companies that will do great things tomorrow are being dreamed up in a dorm room or garage today."

At present the crowd-funding industry is growing very rapidly, and some see it as soon replacing the traditional way that banks serve small businesses. So the question arises whether this type of alternative finance could ultimately replace traditional banking and solve the problems of our boom and bust economy? I think it will at least grow up alongside the traditional system, rather than perhaps replacing it entirely.

Credit unions

In the past few years several credit unions have been started up. They are in some ways just as we imagine banks should be. They are generally owned by their members, and represent a safe and ethical way to save money and borrow it. Credit unions do not borrow money on the money markets, but only lend money out if they have actually received it from depositors. In other words, it is a system of *full-reserve banking*. They have the additional feature that they only receive money locally from people living within a certain area, and they only lend to people from the same area. For example, the Gateway Credit Union, based in Pontypool, only accepts members from Torfaen and Monmouthshire. This means that money lent and borrowed via the credit union effectively stays locally. Credit unions often have representatives visiting local council offices or shops to help people with the administration of their accounts.

Local currencies

Another idea of great interest is that of a local currency. For example, the city of Bristol launched its own currency, called the *Bristol Pound* in September 2012 with a purchasing power equal to one pound Sterling. So far, more than 350 firms in the city have signed up to it, and over 140,000 Bristol pounds (£B) are in circulation, making it the UK's largest alternative to using national currency in the local shops. Unlike previous local currency schemes which have relied on paper notes, the *Bristol Pound* can also be used online and even by mobile phone. The idea is to help local traders by issuing money which customers can only use in their shops. In turn, customers know that the shop must then buy its stock from a local supplier. The new notes contain state-of-the-art security, and feature holograms and gold foil with security numbers etched in by laser. Accounts are held by the Bristol Pound Community Interest Company, partnered by Bristol Credit Union and fully backed by the Financial Services Compensation Scheme.

Fig. 13.2   *A five Bristol Pound note*

However, just three years ago, hopes were equally high in the nearby town of Stroud, which also has a long history of thinking differently. Many hoped the *Stroud Pound* would provide a challenge to global money markets, but today, numbers are down, and only 4,000 *Stroud Pounds* were issued last year, nearly half the level at the launch. Shopkeepers tend to feel the scheme is an accounting nuisance, and the enthusiasm of the volunteers that run the scheme is waning. Bernard Jerman, one of the central people involved, says alternative currencies just need people to get behind them: "*I am a little disappointed because I can see how successful*

---

[39] http://www.bbc.co.uk/news/uk-england-bristol-19627592, article by Dave Harvey, 19th September 2012

it can be in other places, not particularly the UK, because we have this sceptical attitude to money, but abroad they are transforming local economies."[39] Alternative currencies have indeed done well abroad. For example, a currency called the *Chiemgauer* has been operating in Bavaria since 2003. Last year, 550,000 *Chiemgauer* were in circulation, with a turn-over of 6.2 million at an exchange rate of 1:1 with the Euro. In 2006 a rival to the US Dollar was launched in the Berkshire region of Massachusetts, called the *BerkShare*. Since then, 2.2 million have been issued and 370 local firms are signed up.

Barter or trade exchanges

The idea of local currencies brings us neatly to the issue of barter in general. Local currencies are, in a way, a type of bartering, which is still not uncommon amongst individual families in rural communities. People exchange fruit and vegetables with their neighbours, or even meat, poultry and eggs, for example. In general, barter is a system of exchange by which goods or services are directly swapped for other goods or services without using a medium of exchange, such as money. It takes place in parallel to monetary systems, and has historically often replaced money as the method of exchange in times of monetary crisis, such as when a currency becomes unstable or loses its value rapidly (in hyper-inflation). On a commercial level, an organization that provides a trading platform and book-keeping system for, and amongst, its members or clients is called a trade exchange. The member companies buy and sell products and services to each other using an internal currency. Modern barter via trade exchanges has evolved considerably to become an effective method of increasing sales, conserving cash and making use of excess production capacity. Businesses in a barter exchange earn trade credits (instead of cash) that are deposited into their account. They then have the ability to purchase goods and services from other members by using up their trade credits. The exchange provides the record-keeping, brokering expertise and monthly statements to each member. Commercial exchanges make money by charging a commission on each transaction. In the USA there are two groups, the National Association of Trade Exchanges (NATE) and the International Reciprocal Trade Association (IRTA), that offer training and promote high ethical standards among their members. Moreover, each exchange has created its own 'currency' through which its member companies can trade. NATE's currency is known as the BANC, and IRTA's currency is called Universal Currency. The largest trade exchange globally is *Bartercard*, which was founded in Australia in 1991, and now has offices in several countries, including the UK. The very first exchange of this type was the WIR Bank in Switzerland that was founded in 1934 as a result of currency shortages after the stock market crash of 1929. In Spain (particularly Catalonia) a growing number of "literal" exchange markets are appearing. These barter markets work without money. Participants bring things they do not need and exchange them for the unwanted goods of another participant. Swapping among three parties often helps satisfy tastes when trying to get around the rule that money is not allowed. Bartering is good for the environment, and has been encouraged by the environmental movement. The reason for this is that the expenditure of resources involved in the manufacture and distribution of brand-new products is reduced through trading existing products, i.e., it is a form of recycling, and a global market for barter reduces waste and counteracts the "throw-away society". Bartering can thus be regarded as a green alternative to buying and selling goods in a consumer society.

Conclusion

I have merely touched upon a few ways we as individuals can bank ethically. What I mean by that is: only borrow or lend money in such a way as not to make a net increase to the money supply which causes currency erosion, as well as only borrow from or lend to organisations that are involved in environmentally friendly, sustainable or local activities. My recommendation therefore would be either to do business with a green bank, credit union or full-reserve bank, and/or engage in peer-to-peer lending.

Chapter 14: A CHANGE IN PUBLIC ATTITUDE?

"Spend, spend, spend."- Viv Nicholson, who famously won millions of pounds on the football pools in 1962, and spent it all within 4 years, and whose life has been epitomised in a musical of the same name.

Preamble

The dire situation regarding the national debt and the balance of payments deficit is only partly a direct consequence of the government's poor housekeeping. The nub of the problem lies in the way the general public have developed an insatiable desire to "spend, spend, spend", without having the requisite money to do it.

Excessive consumerism

In tandem with the government, each individual household also needs to adopt a frugal policy and reduce its private debt level. This can be achieved by being more selective and discerning in one's consumption. Mass advertising, however, plays a counter rôle, in that it encourages consumers to purchase products they do not really need. I have the impression that school education seems to have failed to instil in individuals a sense of discernment and the objective capability to understand when they are being hoodwinked into buying something they really should not purchase. Many people do not seem to be wise to the fact that if they wait until they can truly afford to buy something, it will effectively cost them less in the long run. For example, since the interest rates on credit card purchases are much higher than the rate of inflation, it is foolish to buy goods with a credit card if they cannot be paid off before interest starts accruing at the over-inflated rate. Usually one has about one month's "grace". Another example: many desirable electronic goods are highly priced when they first come onto the market, but drop in price within a year or two. Does it really matter that we own the very, very latest mobile phone model today? Furthermore, if we were to cut out the nonsense and the superfluous, while being "productive" in our spending (e.g., by buying local strawberries and strawberry plants, instead of importing strawberries from across the globe), gradually the personal debt mountain would disappear.

As expressed in the *Debt Bombshell* website[40]: "*Debt is a strange religion that has come to dominate British life in the post-war era. It teaches that the values of our forebears are outmoded and their achievements of no great significance. It preaches that wealth is no longer created through man's ingenuity and endeavour, but something bestowed upon the grateful congregation by a divine elite. This religion is government, its ministers are politicians and its gospel is debt. Politicians have convinced us that everyone has a right to comfort and happiness and that government has a moral duty to provide it. They believe that wealth and liberation come in the form of paper or electronic money and that distributing limitless amounts of this commodity is a cure for all social and economic ills. However, it is surely obvious that inflating our currency (e.g., by printing more money, as in the euphemistic term quantitative easing), which can reduce the debt burden in the short term, punishes generations of savers and their prudent lives of hard work. Our debt will eventually have to be repaid by our unborn children, while we enrich our lives now at their expense. Our present-day greed is in effect threatening the economic freedom that has enabled more people to improve their material lives than at any other time in the history of mankind.*"

Recent governments have played their part in encouraging excessive consumerism, as have advertising and marketing firms. Politicians, egged on by bankers, have been encouraging consumers to spend more money on non-essential items, allegedly in order for lack of demand not to send the global economy into "freefall". We are told that "consumer confidence" is vital for the recovery of the economy. The socially responsible, even patriotic, thing to do is to go out and spend our money at the sales. And for

---

[40] http://www.debtbombshell.com/

many people, shopping has even become a "social activity" and an "assertion of freedom". It has become a type of "therapy" in a world full of inadequacies and disappointments.

"*But surely we have a right to save our hard-earned money, rather than spend it,*" says Neil Boorman, author of 'Bonfire of the Brands'[41] - who recently made a film to support 'Buy Nothing Day', an annual protest against consumerism. He writes further: "*New cars halve in value the minute we drive them out the showroom, most gadgets become outdated or break down soon after their guarantee expires and clothes are virtually worthless once they are worn. These luxuries are all very exciting when we are carrying them home from the shops, but as investments they're worse bets than Woolworth's shares. Essentially, we are being ripped off. Imagine if we all made a lasting commitment to consuming less - we could pay off those credit cards, save money, even spend less time at work. Faced with the choice - a new car or a four-day week - I know which I would choose. As an anti-consumerism campaigner, I'm frequently labelled as irresponsible when I encourage people to stop shopping. But the government is being much more reckless, when they ask us to shop our way out of the crash. Furthermore, over-consumption is also the root cause of environmental destruction. If ever there was a time to rethink our reliance upon consumerism, when the economic rules are being re-written, it would be now. And it's worth remembering that we used to enjoy a 'buy nothing day' every week of the year. It was called Sunday.*"

Amanda Ford, author of 'Retail Therapy: Life Lessons Learned While Shopping',[42] writes that she has a lot of sympathy for the anti-consumerism campaigners: "*When we spend money on things that we do not need, or for that matter, really even want, we are contributing to a system that negatively impacts our physical environment, our political and social landscapes, and - most importantly, I would argue - our spiritual development. The*

---

[41] "Bonfire of the Brands" by Neil Boorman, published by Canongate Books, Edinburgh (2007)
[42] "Retail Therapy: Life Lessons Learned while Shopping" by Amanda Ford, Conari Press, USA (2003)

answer is to be found in shopping more intelligently," she suggests. "There is absolutely no joy to be found in mindless shopping. 'Less' truly is 'more'. When it comes to consumption, bigger is not better. Does this mean we should shove our money under the mattress and run around wearing clothes crafted of twigs and leaves from our back yards? No. I don't think we need to stop shopping altogether in order to cure our consuming culture, but we do need to shop differently. The idea of lives ruled by shopping and a love of things must be stopped. We must stop purchasing things because we are bored, lonely, stressed or simply going through the motions of obligation and routine. We must support small, local shopkeepers, artisans and farmers. We must buy things that will serve a distinct purpose in our lives for years, not just keep us entertained for a season. People should continue shopping, but do it with the state of the world at the back of their minds. We must not be afraid to spend our money. Money is a tremendous force and even a little bit has power to create positive change. Every time you shop, ask yourself, 'Does this purchase support or negate the type of change I want to see in the world? Is this purchase life-affirming or soul-draining.' Then take a deep breath, centre yourself and listen. I think you will know your answer."

On the other hand, there are those who defend luxury spending as an inalienable right, and refer to austerity measures as like having to live under the Pol Pot regime in Cambodia or the Taliban in Afghanistan. Lucia van der Post, for example, founder of the Financial Times' glossy magazine 'How to Spend It', says that "*in a capitalist society people should be able to spend money that they've earned and paid tax on, on whatever they like. Fun is an essential to us all - as essential as food and water. I am fundamentally libertarian. I will never be able to afford a yacht but I like to live in a world where some people have yachts. Do we want a world where no-one knows how to make a yacht or a fine watch?*"

It would certainly be nice to have all the latest electronic gadgets, a big 4x4 car, designer clothes, exotic fruit, and the most expensive kitchen in the catalogue. I don't blame anyone for wanting these sorts of things, and I can understand why they "want it all and want it now"! However, the analysts, whether they are for or against consumerism, all fail to point out the crucial fact that British industry is not capable of satisfying this enormous buying urge. The consequence is that far too many goods have to be imported, instead of being produced or manufactured in this country. Our manufacturing industry has floundered and declined painfully over many decades, while successive Westminster governments – both Labour and Conservative – have watched and failed to stem the tide.[43]

However, all is not lost, because Britain's economic problems could be gradually solved by a voluntary change in public attitude. Nothing positive will be achieved, however, until each member of the general public realises that he or she personally needs to contribute to improving the economic state of the country, rather than expecting the government to solve all the problems for them.

The economic figures outlined in the previous chapters tell us quite clearly that – at this particular point in our history – it is essential to reduce imports. In this respect the government and the Bank of England have their hands tied, for they can only "tweak" taxes and interest rates. They are not allowed, in particular by European Law, to put up trade barriers or impose import duty or other restrictions. In any case, this would be a mistake, since history tells us that it would be counter-productive, causing a run on our currency and frightening off potential foreign investment.

The only answer is for the general public themselves to do something about it. Britain's annual trade deficit of more than £50bn means that each person on average is buying too many foreign goods to the value of at least £830 per year. This is quite a lot of money for an average household: £2,000, but here are some suggestions:

---

[43] I have, however, noticed a positive trend locally, in Wales, where it seems that the Assembly Government has been doing all it can to encourage manufacturing businesses to locate in depressed areas.

WAR ON DEBT

Buying a car (or any other large item)

In the glossy showroom, nothing is further from one's mind than the fact that buying a foreign car means supporting jobs abroad and not here - and that by purchasing a foreign car one is contributing to the UK's balance of payments deficit. But if you purchase a car manufactured in the UK instead of a foreign one then you and your family have done your bit for several years – and you can go off and buy whatever else you fancy, without having a guilty conscience![44]

In the supermarket

The Archbishop of York, John Sentamu, as well as many others, has suggested that we should place more emphasis on buying British food. For the average parent frequenting a food supermarket each week, *not* to buy £40 worth of imported food (£2,000 divided by the number of weeks in a year) that you would normally buy is a tough challenge – but you might manage not to purchase the sea bass from the other side of the world, and try something from British waters, lakes or rivers instead. Admittedly, it is nice to have strawberries at Christmas time, but you don't *need* to have them flown in from the southern hemisphere. Why not wait, and buy local ones in June? You'll enjoy them all the more. And instead of those runner beans from across the water, you can surely get local ones from the farmers' market.

The easiest way to cut down on imported food is to buy local produce directly from farm shops, farmers' markets or local grocers' shops - even if local produce might be slightly more expensive; it might also be cheaper. If a product does not have a label on it stating its origin, then always ask the vendor where it comes from. If enough supermarket customers are discerning about the origin of the products they buy, then the supermarkets

---

[44] This example is obviously very simplistic, because a car assembled in the UK may contain a large proportion of foreign components. Similarly, a foreign car may contain components made here – especially when it comes to global companies, such as Ford. A British company like Vauxhall, owned by GM of America, may well have had some of its cars produced in Germany by another daughter company of GM, Opel.

will be forced to buy non-imported produce. Until the consumer demands British produce, the seller will continue to offer imported goods for sale.

Cutting back on spending

You don't have to *buy* everything. You can be creative and do many things for yourself, for example, plant your own vegetables. If you have no garden, you can probably rent an allotment, or put pots of tomatoes, peppers, etc. on the balcony or patio. It doesn't save much money, but it will probably give you a sense of satisfaction. Make some of your own furniture. Don't waste money driving your car unnecessarily; take a bus, cycle, or walk instead. If you have to go by car, then try to arrange a car-sharing network. Being frugal is a good way to reduce imports, because you are not participating in the consumer epidemic. However, this doesn't necessarily help the local economy a great deal.

Clearly, it is only feasible to buy non-imported goods if an equivalent British product is readily available. Most consumer electronic items are now only manufactured abroad, so they will have to be imported until measures are taken to manufacture them here as well. Some items (and most raw materials for industry) have to be imported – and there is absolutely nothing wrong with that. But it is not difficult to make a conscious effort to "Buy British". If large numbers of consumers did this as a matter of course, not only would the balance of payments deficit problem soon be brought under control, but British industry would automatically be stimulated and unemployment reduced.

The above suggestions should not be regarded as protectionist, for the simple reason that no tariffs, trade barriers or tax advantages are involved, and there is certainly nothing illegal about them – they are simply common sense. The fact is that people in every other major industrialised country consciously and patriotically purchase their own indigenous products as their first choice. Why do the British not do the same? The main reason today is that we are swamped for choice from the global market.

It must be said as well that it is now almost impossible to gauge the true origin of most products, since we live in this global market. For example, even ostensibly British vacuum cleaners made by the British company Dyson are manufactured abroad to keep labour costs low and the company competitive – and this aspect is clearly problematical for UK industry.

On the subject of competitiveness, Marks & Spencer used proudly to claim that all their goods were manufactured in the UK, but at some point in the past they abandoned that principle, due to the uncompetitiveness of British textile goods. Britain is currently being swamped by clothing from some of the developing countries: attractively cheap articles "dumped" in this country, having been manufactured in the "sweatshops" of Asia. Highly sophisticated electronic and household goods are also flooding the UK market, in particular from China. They are generally of very good quality and remarkably inexpensive, and it is highly tempting to buy them - I am using a computer that has been imported from somewhere in Asia, in order to be able to write this book! I'm not suggesting we boycott foreign goods, just that we shop with discernment. But it does seem rather silly to purchase Christmas cards and books that have been made, for example, in China, when we can quite easily print them ourselves in this country.

Could we pay off the national debt?

If the present ND could be erased, the Exchequer would have an extra £30-40 billion each year to use legitimately! So, would it be possible to pay off the ND?

Why is it that successive governments consistently fall into the same trap that ensnares feckless individuals, viz. living beyond their means and overspending? Everyone surely knows that borrowing money is short-sighted and that you are ultimately worse off because of having to pay excess interest, than if you can manage without borrowing. The money you borrow is essentially paying the salaries of the money lenders! Unless money is being borrowed to make a substantial improvement in efficiency or increase in production, then it is not worth considering.

But this is one of the age-old problems facing UK governments in general – they are forced to be short-sighted. They dare not cut public services radically, in order to save money, because the public would complain, there would be unrest, and the government would become unpopular and lose support. If the government raised taxes to increase revenue, this would also be unpopular. Politicians who want to remain elected are therefore inherently forced to act in their own personal interests, not in the interests of the country as a whole.

Where, then, are the checks on government we should have in our parliamentary democracy? Why does Parliament not prevent the Executive (i.e., the Chancellor in his budget) from overspending? Where does the judiciary stand in all of this? Why is it not a legal requirement for the Chancellor of the Exchequer to balance his books each year? He should only be allowed to spend what he receives in tax revenue. This would be a very hard, short, sharp lesson for the country, but I am sure it would soon bear fruit.

What then is the solution to this enormous problem of national debt? Some lateral thinking is required. Perhaps there needs to be a concerted effort to help the government – an act of solidarity by the general public.

Should the government impose an additional tax dedicated directly to paying off the ND? Unfortunately, people would not take kindly to any tax of this kind, mainly because of an inherent distrust of government to do this properly. So, what about voluntary contributions? If enough people participated in a voluntary scheme, they could make a real impact in reducing the national debt. However, there is no consensus at present indicating that this needs to be done; in fact, hardly anybody is aware of the severity of the problem.

In any case, newspapers and the media are constantly complaining about the high level of taxes in this country. On the one hand, the government is being urged to lower taxes, but, on the other hand, it has to provide ever-improving health care, education and social services. The government is virtually being coerced by public opinion to get around this problem by relinquishing its own responsibilities and leaving more and more to the private sector to sort out. Instead of paying higher taxes, we find ourselves taking out insurance policies for various services, such as private medical and dental care, or we pay out of our own pockets, or we have to take out loans to pay for higher education, instead of it being funded largely by the state. This way of doing things doesn't make us any better off!

However, it should be pointed out that not everyone thinks taxes are necessarily too high. Realistically we have to pay for the services we receive – but taxes do need to be fair, and a lot of argument revolves around how much higher earners should pay. As I shall propose later in this chapter, the way taxes are implemented needs to be transparent, so that people know exactly where their precious money is being used. How much does the NHS cost, for example? What NI contribution, via percentage of salary, needs to be levied in order to cover that cost?

National Savings

If I felt I could trust the government to use our money wisely, I would be happy to pay higher taxes to pay off the national debt; in fact, I would be prepared to pay approximately £20,000 (over a period of time) to pay off my personal contribution to the ND – under the proviso, of course, that everyone else did the same!

However, since we are living in the real world, we probably need to think of another way to solve this type of debt problem. For instance, why does the government not set up an institution where anyone can invest their excess cash, gain some interest, and where the profits go towards paying off the national debt?

This idea is, of course, not at all new: it is called a nationalised savings bank. But don't we already have in public possession a few nationalised banks: Lloyds, RBS? Why privatise them again?

Moreover we already do have a type of national savings bank called National Savings and Investments (NS&I)! Paraphrasing NS&I's own website: The Post Office Savings Bank – as the NS&I was originally called when Lord Palmerston set it up in 1861 – was a savings scheme aimed at encouraging wage earners to provide savings against adversity and ill health. The scheme quickly became popular and the deposits found their way from the Post Office to the Exchequer, providing a fund which the Chancellor, William Gladstone, could borrow to use towards public spending. Its two principles, which have remained in place ever since, are to provide a totally secure place backed by the Government for people to save, and to provide the Exchequer with a source of funding. Significant expansion over the next century included the introduction of Savings Certificates during the First World War to help finance the war effort, while Premium Bonds were launched for sale in 1956 by Harold Macmillan, the Chancellor of the Exchequer at the time. 1969 saw the first main structural change - the Post Office Savings Bank became a separate government department accountable to Treasury ministers, and was renamed National Savings. The Post Office now just supports NS&I's business as a distribution outlet for its products. In 1996 National Savings became an Executive Agency of the Chancellor of the Exchequer. In February 2002 the organisation became known as National Savings & Investments, and later this was shortened to NS&I. While NS&I remains accountable to the Treasury, agency status has given it greater autonomy in day-to-day management.

In other words, what used to be a nationalised savings bank is now run more or less as a private commercial company, and since 1999 its operations have been controlled largely by the company Siemens IT Solutions and Services. The Treasury still uses money invested in NS&I, however, to manage the national debt "cost-effectively" (as it calls it). At present, NS&I has 27 million customers who have invested £94 billion pounds. I cannot honestly judge whether or not the present 'Public Private Partnership' set-up of NS&I represents a good deal for the British public and the Treasury, but I suspect not.

Supporting British manufacturing

One of the factors contributing to an increasing level of unemployment has been the decline in industrial production. What is meant by production here is the total output, which includes the manufacturing of goods as well as the output of industries such as the mining and oil industries. One talks about oil and gas *production* but, to be more precise, oil and gas are not actually produced; they are extracted from the ground. Anyway, whenever production has dropped, unemployment has risen. An official measure of production in the UK is the 'Index of Production' shown in the next graph.

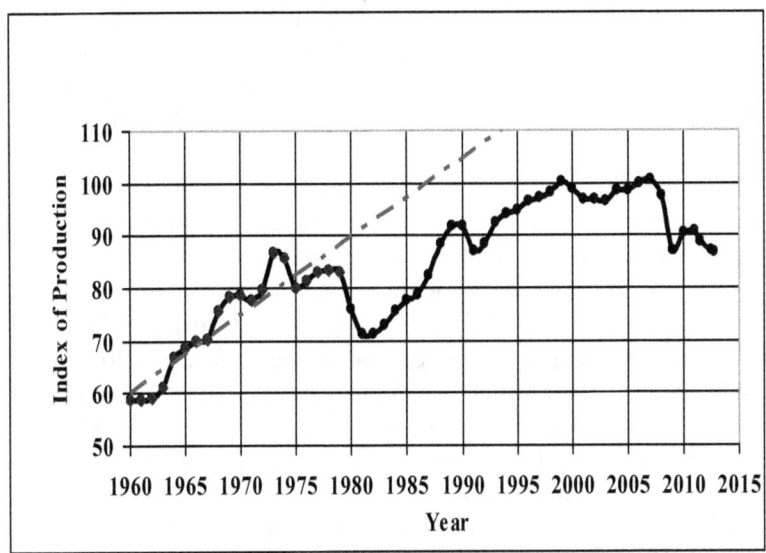

Fig.14.1: Index of Production (Data source: ONS) (2006 = 100)

This index has been discussed in detail in my previous book[45], so I shall only summarise some important aspects here. There is a steady increase in production all the way from just after the end of WW2 (not shown here) up until the peak in 1973, followed by a dip caused by the Oil Crisis, when there was an embargo on oil by Arab states, such that we did not have enough of this commodity to run our industry fully. The year 1980, though, marks the most

---

[45] *"So Many False Dawns in British Poliitics"*, A.J.Owen (2010), published by AJBooks, Monmouth, UK

significant change caused by influences *internal* to this country: Margaret Thatcher began restructuring the UK's publicly-owned enterprises in preparation for eventual privatisation. This resulted in a massive 15% drop in production between 1979 and 1981. The subsequent increase towards the end of the 1980s was achieved largely from the burgeoning oil and gas extraction out of the North Sea, not from efficiency or productivity improvements in existing industry. The graph also shows the effect of a recession in 1990. The most recent recession beginning in 2009 is manifested by the large dip to the right of the graph, where output dropped by about 13% in just over a year. The year 2010 saw a small recovery in output, but more recently industrial output has been decreasing again.

The trend line on the graph calculated from 1960 to 1979 shows that production was increasing by about 2% per annum on average over that period. Continuing the trend line beyond 1979, we see what might have been achieved in production if Mrs Thatcher had not privatised Britain's public enterprises! The Index of Production might well have been in the region of 120 or even much higher today, rather than languishing near 90. This is surely convincing evidence, even proof, that the wholescale privatisation of British industry was a disaster for the country, and that the benefits of privatisation are a myth that has been engendered by those who have a vested interest in it.

It is clear that industrial output needs to rise again. Specifically, the decline in Britain's manufacturing industries needs to be reversed significantly, but how can it be achieved? Primarily, the government needs to show much more support for manufacturing. However, unfortunately, the Coalition is not doing enough in this area. For example, although it has been supporting the British rail industry, the £1.4 billion government contract for carriages for the new Thameslink has been awarded to the German company Siemens, as opposed to the company Bombardier, which would have manufactured the carriages in Derby. Losing the contract means that Bombardier, the last manufacturer in the rail industry in the UK, will shed 1,400 employees or about 50% of its workforce in Derby, and many more skilled jobs will be lost in the supply chain. The Prime Minister in a meeting with Derbyshire MPs (July 2011) insisted that the decision cannot be changed, because it is legally bound to continue the Thameslink project with German engineering firm Siemens as the preferred bidder. Who made the decision and signed the contract in the first place, I wonder? This raises the issue of 'public versus private' ownership again, of course, for the works in Derby – now owned by Bombardier – used to be publicly owned, as was British Rail. There would have been no question in the past about who would win the contract to build the carriages.

This directly reminds me of very significant political discussions that took place, as it happens, in Germany, about thirty years ago. Faced with the increasing quantity of cheap imports from countries such as China as well as from eastern Europe, politicians engaged the public in discussing the importance of their country retaining its strong manufacturing base. Politicians pledged they would do all they could to keep Germany manufacturing, despite the pressure from abroad. They succeeded using measures that could be regarded as bordering on protectionist – but I think were probably legal according to European Law – and Germany became the largest exporter of manufactured goods in the world (possibly overtaken only this year by China). Meanwhile, in the UK, we had the Thatcher government, in conflict with the trade unions, presiding over the dismantling of British industry. Thus, I think it is important for the present coalition government to do its utmost to reverse this decline. They need to do the same as the German government did several decades ago, and get the conditions right for an economic miracle in this country right now.

One of the hindrances to this, I'm afraid, is that both UK politicians and the general public as a whole have been quite ignorant about the importance of UK-based manufacturing, and the link between industrial production, engineering and science education. There is also a marked lack of practical skills and qualifications amongst the British workforce compared to those in many other developed nations. There is an insufficient number of people training here as apprentices, learning their trade properly and gaining master qualifications. In his recent budget statement, however, George Osborne has tried to alleviate this problem by announcing there will be an additional 20,000 apprenticeships funded over the next two years. In addition, there will be 30,000 extra student places in 2014-15, as well as increased funding for science, technology and engineering courses.

I find it exceedingly frustrating to discover that when I go to a large store, I am unable to find any products that have been manufactured in this country, in particular white goods and electronic equipment. Do we really want to go back to being a society of "hunter-gatherers", where we roam the countryside looking for berries to eat? If we do not get a grip soon, that is what will gradually happen, as the country becomes increasingly poor and bereft of technical skills. Educated people will continue to leave the country to find skilled jobs elsewhere in the world where engineering and technology are given a much higher priority. Our present-day affluence is unsustainable, since it is based on debt. We have to turn round and earn our high standard of living ourselves, before it is too late.

Protecting and creating employment

There is no doubt that jobs must be protected, and new ones created. Over two million unemployed are already far too many. There is no sense in having millions of idle, unproductive people in the country, living off state benefits. Not only is it financially and psychologically bad for them and their families, it is also expensive for the taxpayer: the amount of "dead money" the government has to give away on state benefits will only decrease if more people find employment. In other words, more jobs mean decreased social security spending (an obvious fact). In addition, this will increase government revenue through income tax, as well as VAT through increased consumer spending. Thus, an increased level of employment should be an absolute priority. However, you do not create jobs simply by throwing money randomly at the economy, which is in effect what the Bank of England has been doing recently via QE.

However, there is something that is rarely mentioned about the job situation that should at least be touched upon here. A friend of mine once remarked: "*I don't mind working; what I don't like is having a job*", or words to that effect. Having a job in some companies and under some managements can be a desultory experience. Working conditions in the UK are generally not very amenable, partly because of class attitudes, such as the "them and us" mentality. Furthermore, the quality of jobs seems to be becoming increasingly poor as skilled or trained manufacturing workers are increasingly having to turn to doing repetitive or monotonous work in modern-day sweatshops, such as call centres and retail warehouses, where there is virtually no feeling of community spirit. We generally have a hierarchical structure of accountability where people have to assess their juniors; jobs can be monotonous and stressful, and people are often forced to work very long and antisocial hours. All this deters many people from holding down or even wanting a job. To take people fully out of unemployment, it is therefore necessary for the work ambience to be more sensitive to people's needs. Teamwork is far better than hierarchy, so that people feel more equal in worth within their organisation, and not as if they are tantamount to being just a modern-day slave subservient to, and exploited by, some imperious master. In other words we need to get rid of class inequality in the workplace, as well as income inequality.

Linked to employment - or employability - is also the fact that there is something seriously wrong with the educational system in the UK - as many people will be able to tell you. I do not want to point the blame here at any particular aspect, but I shall just mention a few salient points. The recent *PISA* results have of course highlighted that much is left to be desired, and it does seem that many young people seem to have "lost the plot" when it comes to their own education, compared to young people in many other countries, especially those in Asia. Too many UK children are leaving school unmotivated and without proper qualifications. To try to correct that deficiency, it has just been announced by the Chancellor in his Autumn Statement (December 2013) that anyone aged 18 to 21 claiming benefits without basic english or mathematics skills will be required to take training, and people unemployed for 6 months will be forced to start a traineeship, take work experience or do community work placement, if they wish to retain their entitlement to benefits.

The reason jobseekers need to carry out some focussed activity is that it is very damaging to one's self-esteem to remain idle for long. Being unemployed temporarily, however, can actually give one a chance to rethink one's life and learn new skills while having a genuine career break. Personally, I think everyone in employment should have the statutory right periodically to take sabbatical leave (not just university professors). It is also worth pointing out that a massive amount of voluntary (unpaid) work is carried out in this country by retired people who have the experience and capability to continue doing some work as they get older.

Stimulating the economy

Orthodox capitalist thinking deems low interest rates to be necessary in order to "crank up" or stimulate the economy to prevent the country slipping back into recession, but why should this actually work? Is it an efficient way to promote economic activity, or are there better ways? In principle, with low interest rates, businesses should feel able to borrow extra capital, since loan interest payments would be relatively low. This money is then invested in the business to buy new machinery and premises, which should in theory increase productivity and output.

However, in the current situation in the UK this does not necessarily create new jobs or protect the jobs that already exist. At present, the UK's manufacturing capabilities really have diminished below a healthy threshold, and most equipment needed by companies to increase productivity generally comes from abroad. With borrowed money a firm could theoretically buy robots from Japan, which would be used to replace some of the existing workforce! Benefiting from this will be the company in Japan making the robots, and possibly the directors and shareholders of the business, if it leads to higher profits. This is a hypothetical (yet realistic) example of a situation where stimulating the economy actually has a negative effect, i.e., it is counter-productive with regard to employment in the UK as well as being bad for the UK's balance of payments, unless the company exports most of its products. I think this is a very common situation. It is therefore dangerous and naïve to stimulate the economy without direction or planning. The stimulation needs to be directed or regulated not only into capital investment but also into "homespun" manufacturing. In the above example, it would only be effective if the robots themselves were manufactured in the UK in which case jobs might be created in the company producing robots. The government does not seem to realise that stimulating the economy in an unfocussed way inevitably leads to a higher balance of payments deficit, and not necessarily to more jobs in the UK.

In addition, costs can often be reduced by outsourcing manufacturing to foreign countries – meaning importing the manufactured goods back to this country, e.g., Dyson vacuum cleaners are made in Malaysia, for an ostensibly British company. All this needs to change. Dyson vacuum cleaners for the UK market also need to be manufactured here in the UK, not in Malaysia.

How do you achieve that? Banks should lend money to firms willing to manufacture here, but not to firms that are intending to acquire their equipment from abroad. How can this be regulated in an internationally legal way in a global economy with privately operated banks? The answer is that banks that are already nationalised must be kept under public control. Now that they have been bailed out using taxpayers' money, they should be run for the benefit of the taxpayer, and not re-privatised. It is time for the government again to act like a responsible business on behalf of the British public. If private banks can make huge profits for their shareholders, so can publicly owned banks make huge profits for the taxpayer, thus reducing the tax burden and government deficit.

It is therefore foolish in practice for the government to use this low-interest-rate stimulation model. It might be appropriate in a country such as Germany which manufactures most of its engineering products itself, but it will not work effectively in a country such as the UK that relies too much on imported technical goods. Thus, investing borrowed money in a company is a double-edged sword. It needs to be done wisely for the good of the workforce, not at its expense. Instead of borrowing money irresponsibly, businesses should expand equably by using their operating profits to invest in modernisation. In practice, however, operating profits are often paid out as bonuses to directors, instead of being ploughed back into the company as they should be.

Unfortunately, it has become eminently clear that unfettered capitalism here at home and on a global scale, with its lack of regulation and excessive debt burden, is the primary cause of the demise exacerbating the UK's ailing economy. There must be a way forward for the UK, however, but we need to rid ourselves of a certain amount of political and economic baggage. The Conservative doctrine that free enterprise holds the key to success and affluence is misguided. It has, and will, inevitably fail, because it relies far too much on the power and greed of the individual as its driving force. It leads to increasing unfairness and inequality: there are more "haves and have-nots" now in this country as a result of it over the past thirty years. What we do need is a society in which hard work is rewarded <u>and</u> vulnerable people are protected. To achieve this, the government itself needs to step in proactively and run a significant and strategic part of the economy as a well-organised business for the benefit of all its stakeholders, i.e., you and me.

Social market economy

In West Germany in the 1970s and 80s, a social market economy, as implemented by the Social Democratic Party (SDP) of Helmut Schmidt and Willi Brandt with their coalition partner, the Free Democrats (or Liberals), under Dietrich Genscher, did seem to incorporate the best of both worlds in many respects, i.e., it was both socially responsible and market orientated. This also applies to most of the German ways of doing things that have ensued in the intervening years. There is a down-to-earth sense of cost and value there, and a belief that problems can be solved properly. Let us take healthcare as an example. The ordinary citizen in Germany knows exactly how much he or she contributes specifically to health insurance, and what services they are entitled to. A German pensioner, for example, has 7.0% of his/her earnings-related pension deducted for healthcare contributions and 0.85% for compulsory care insurance. It sounds a lot, and it is, but the service is very good. In the UK, on the other hand, the general public have no idea of the cost of the healthcare provided by the National Health Service. For this reason, there is the tendency for people here to think that free healthcare is somehow their birthright, i.e., an entitlement that costs nothing. But who does pay for it, and how much? Good question. Of course, in the UK there is the vague belief that some proportion of National Insurance contributions is used to pay for it, but how the required money is allocated exactly to the health service from taxes is a mystery that does not interest anyone. However, when NI contributions have to be raised, as recently, it would be helpful to know what purpose they will be put to. It might make people realise that it is unrealistic to expect something for nothing. In other words, the government would do well to separate out the cost of NHS contributions from pension and unemployment contributions. The majority of us would be quite surprised at how little we pay for healthcare compared to German citizens (9.6% of GDP as opposed to 11.6%) – and as a consequence not surprised at the present shortcomings of the NHS. We would then have to decide how much we are actually prepared to pay, and if the consensus is that we want a better service, then we would need to pay higher contributions.

Apart from medical care itself, there is the issue of care for the elderly. In the UK it is hard to know who actually foots the bill, and how much the individual has to contribute via means testing towards a place in a care home. Rumours abound that some people have to sell their homes in order to be looked after, while others transfer the ownership of their homes and their savings to relatives in order to evade having to pay for their care. It is a situation lacking in transparency in this country and fraught with fear for the people involved. However, in Germany there is a compulsory state insurance requiring contributions of 1.7% of income, shared between employer and employee, which by and large sorts out this care issue in its entirety. What Britain needs now is a politician with vision equivalent to the German CDU politician, Norbert Blüm, who almost single-handedly devised and got through their parliament the immensely important bill setting up the system of care insurance in Germany some twenty years ago.

Conclusion

With the first coalition government in office in the UK within living memory, we may be experiencing a revived kind of consensus politics. With increased powers and responsibilities for the devolved nations of the UK, we may be seeing a gradual shift of financial power away from the City of London to regional capitals. As a result of the ongoing financial crisis, we might be able to achieve a radical reform of the banking system and a new way of thinking about wealth and money, as well as a more balanced economy. The balance, however, must be on at least three different levels: firstly, a balanced budget is necessary; secondly, we need to have a balance between manufacturing and service industries, since at present our economy is dominated by the service industries. Thirdly, there needs to be a balance between exports and imports, i.e., the trade deficit needs to be eliminated by decreasing our reliance on imported goods. Then, and only then, can we say we have a healthy and sustainable economy. These should be the aims and economic priorities of the present government.

However, the public itself needs to play a much larger rôle. We as ordinary individuals need to free ourselves from the clutches of the big manipulators, viz., the media and the banks, or at least regulate their influence on us and society more strictly, for they are only using us for their own ends. We need to recognise where the advertising media are encouraging us to spend money unnecessarily, and where the press and television are indoctrinating us into self-centred and superficial lifestyles. Politicians - whom I shall define as public servants running the country on our behalf - cannot be relied upon to do everything right for the community as a whole, so we proactively need to advise and hold to account those in government, all the way from local level to the corridors of power in Westminster.

Furthermore, there needs to be a change in public attitude – in many ways a reversion to old-fashioned principles of good house-keeping, hard work, debt-free frugality, purchasing locally, as well as care and concern for the environment and the vulnerable members of our society. Rather than spending our entire lives fruitlessly seeking personal gain and just "feathering our own nests" (activities which do not bring happiness), each individual needs to focus on what he or she can do personally to serve the community in a positive way (which does bring happiness), the sum total of which will then bring about a radical change for the better in our society. This message applies to everyone.

Acknowledgments

I should like to thank my wife, Ruth, for painstakingly proofreading and improving the text; any mistakes remaining, however, are entirely my own fault. Thanks are also due to Lionel Demery for helpful suggestions.

www.ingramcontent.com/pod-product-compliance
Lightning Source LLC
Chambersburg PA
CBHW060859170526
45158CB00001B/426